A Man Named Joseph

A Man Named
JOSEPH

Guardian for Our Times

JOE HESCHMEYER

Our Sunday Visitor
Huntington, Indiana

Nihil Obstat
Msgr. Michael Heintz, Ph.D.
Censor Librorum

Imprimatur
✠ Kevin C. Rhoades
Bishop of Fort Wayne-South Bend
March 25, 2021

The *Nihil Obstat* and *Imprimatur* are official declarations that a book is free from doctrinal or moral error. It is not implied that those who have granted the *Nihil Obstat* and *Imprimatur* agree with the contents, opinions, or statements expressed.

Our Sunday Visitor Publishing Division, Our Sunday Visitor, Inc., 200 Noll Plaza, Huntington, IN 46750; www.osv.com; 1-800-348-2440

ISBN: 978-1-68192-952-1 (Inventory No. T2687)
1. RELIGION—Christianity—Saints & Sainthood.
2. RELIGION—Christianity—Catholic.
3. RELIGION—Christian Theology—General.

eISBN: 978-1-68192-953-8
LCCN: 2021933407

Cover design/interior design: Amanda Falk
Cover art: AdobeStock
PRINTED IN THE UNITED STATES OF AMERICA

To J. S.:
May God guide you,
through the intercession of
Saint Joseph

Contents

Author's Note

The obvious difficulty with writing a book about Saint Joseph is that his name appears only fourteen times in Scripture, and he's never quoted directly. As a result, there are two temptations that authors can easily fall into. The first is to become overly imaginative, telling readers, on the basis of the authors' speculation, what "must have" happened. The second is to supplement the New Testament data with other material, such as private revelation or noncanonical writings.

I've consciously tried to resist both of these temptations, for two reasons. First, I wanted this book to have as broad an appeal as possible. It's unmistakably the work of a Catholic author, but the vast majority of the book should be accessible to any Christian prepared to accept the authority of the Bible. Even when (as frequently happens) I quote popes or

saints, it's because I think that they have something insight-
ful to say on the scriptural portrait of Saint Joseph. Second,
I think it's important to hone in on the scriptural picture of
Joseph, because I'm convinced (and I hope to help show)
that there's a lot more there than first meets the eye, and that
we've misunderstood his story in some profound ways.

1.

The Hidden Saint

In the Gospel of Luke, Jesus tells a parable about a marriage feast. He concludes with the admonition that "when you are invited, go and sit in the lowest place, so that when your host comes he may say to you, 'Friend, go up higher'; then you will be honored in the presence of all who sit at table with you. For every one who exalts himself will be humbled, and he who humbles himself will be exalted" (Lk 14:10–11). Perhaps no saint in history has better exemplified this journey from the lowest place than Jesus' foster-father, Saint Joseph.

Saint Joseph has been aptly described as "the man closest to Jesus."[1] Yet, for most of the Church's history, he languished in obscurity. Pope Saint John XXIII referred to Joseph as "the most hidden of all the saints of God,"[2] and described how, "except for some slight sprinkling of references to him here and there in the writings of the Fathers," he spent many centuries "in the background that was so typical of him, like a kind of ornamental detail in the overall picture of the Savior's life."[3] We might think of Joseph almost like the ox in the Nativity scene that is — brought out for a few weeks in Advent and then put back into storage after Christmas.

This centuries-long general neglect existed at the levels of both popular devotion and serious theology. Joseph remains virtually ignored in the writings of the Church Fathers, in early Christian prayers, and even in the Liturgy. It's only in the twelfth century that we begin to see churches and altars named after him, and he wasn't given a feast day on the universal liturgical calendar until 1479.[4] Part of the reason for this may have been that he died before the public ministry of Jesus. He did his work in quiet obscurity in Nazareth and then died, long before anyone realized just who the boy whom he had raised truly was. Additionally, he didn't die a martyr's death. In the early days of the Church, while persecutions were either ongoing or still fresh in the Christian imagination, it was the martyrs who (unsurprisingly) were generally the favorite saints.[5]

Another reason for Joseph's obscurity may be that Scripture itself is virtually silent about him. Given the important role that he undoubtedly played as the foster-father of Jesus, we are told surprisingly little about him, and we hear even less from him. Were it not for Matthew 1:25 (in which we read that Joseph fulfilled the angel's instructions to name the child Jesus), we would have no record of him speaking at all. This left, for many Christians, the question of just what sort of man Saint Joseph was.

Unfortunately, both popular literature and medieval theater filled these gaps by presenting Joseph "as a doddering ancient, an unwilling spouse and a jealous husband, whose conviction that his wife had committed adultery inspired scenes a good deal more lively than those of the Nativity itself."[6] In short, he was represented as a man who could hardly serve as an inspiration for theological treatises or devout prayers.

Religious paintings and iconography were scarcely better. Given the "scant literary description" of Saint Joseph, early Christian artists were faced with a problem: How were they to depict Joseph as the "protector to the child and mother," while still suggesting to the (perhaps illiterate or uninformed) viewer that he wasn't the biological father of Jesus?[7] The results were often to make Joseph look peeved, anxious, or sad. For instance, in ancient English art, "the most common image of the Nativity from the sixth century on shows a cave, with Mary reclining on a couch, the child in an altarlike manger with the ox and ass on either side, and a seated Joseph resting his head on his hand. Joseph's head is often averted from the child, probably as a means of expressing that he is not the father."[8]

Perhaps it's no wonder, then, that there was little enthusiasm for Saint Joseph for so long. But the man who assumes the lowest place at the table is eventually told, "Friend, go up higher," to be honored in the presence of the rest of the guests. For Joseph, that turning point arguably came in 1416 when Jean Gerson, chancellor of the University of Paris, argued before the Council of Constance that the Church needed to honor Saint Joseph.[9] The next year, Gerson, "one of the most important and influential figures in the history of the devotion to Saint Joseph,"[10] published a lengthy (three-thousand hexameter!) Latin poem about Saint Joseph called the *Josephina*, which quickly drew the hearts of believers to the great saint.[11]

As Pope Saint John XXIII recounted, "It took time for devotion to him to go beyond those passing glances and take root in the hearts of the faithful, and then surge forth in the form of special prayers and of a profound sense of trust and confidence."[12] But surge it did. Over the next two hundred years, with the help of Saint Teresa of Ávila and Saint Francis de Sales, Joseph became one of the most beloved saints in the Church.[13] It is hard to overstate the height to which God has raised Joseph these past six centuries. On December 8, 2020, in calling a Year of Saint Joseph, Pope Francis observed that "after Mary, the Mother of God, no saint is mentioned more frequently in the papal magisterium than Joseph, her spouse."[14] That's quite the turnaround for a saint once ignored, or written off as a doddering old fool. As his wife would say, God "has put down the mighty from their thrones, / and exalted those of low degree" (Lk 1:52).

But how this remarkable reversal happened is of less importance than why. What is it that Saint Joseph has to offer the Church — and each one of us — today? That's the question that this book seeks to answer. To get there, we'll have to cut through a lot of our own misconceptions to see what the Bible and the earliest Christians have to say about Joseph as a model husband, father, and saint. Before that, though, we need to address a more fundamental question: Why should we care about Saint Joseph at all?

PRAYER
At the end of each chapter in this book, I'll include a short prayer to Saint Joseph that you can offer so that this book is a work of the heart and not simply the head. To begin, here's the prayer with which Pope Saint John XXIII entrusted the Church to the protection of Saint Joseph as he opened the Second Vatican Council.[15] As we pray it today, look at the

features of Joseph's spirituality that John XXIII highlights, and see where you could most use his intercession:

> Always be our protector. May thy inner spirit of peace, of silence, of good work, and of prayer for the cause of Holy Church always be an inspiration to us and bring us joy in union with thy blessed spouse, our most sweet and gentle and Immaculate Mother, and in the strong yet tender love of Jesus, the glorious and immortal King of all ages and peoples. Amen.

QUESTIONS

1. In my life, do I try to claim the "highest place" for myself by making sure that people notice and praise the good things that I do (as a Christian, at my job, and within my family)?

2. How do I respond when I seem to be in the "lowest place" or feel unjustly overlooked? What can I learn from Saint Joseph in this regard?

3. Why might the Church have initially "forgotten" Joseph?

4. What circumstances might have led to the Church's "remembering" Joseph in recent centuries, and what can this remembering tell us about our situation as Christians today?

2.

Patron of the Universal Church

If you want to make sense of Saint Joseph, the first thing you have to know about him is that you can understand him only in light of two other people: Mary and Jesus. Literally every detail that we know about him is in reference to one or both of them. This isn't a coincidence or owing simply to the fact that there is so little recorded of him in Scripture. Rather, this is the hallmark of sanctity: As John the Baptist said, "He must increase, but I must decrease" (Jn 3:30). We draw near to Saint Joseph precisely because he draws us near not to himself but to Jesus, just as we draw near to Mary precisely because she says, "Do whatever he [Jesus] tells you" (Jn 2:5).

Critics of the Catholic Church's emphasis on the saints, and particularly on the Virgin Mary, tend to miss this point. One anti-Catholic book presents the argument this way: "God's Word repeatedly instructs you to look to the eternal God of the universe as your model and source of holiness. Catholicism counters, saying, 'No, don't look to God, look to this frail, human woman.' This is nothing short of blasphemy."[1] Of course, Catholicism *doesn't* say not to look to God. But it *does* say that we should look to the saints (and particularly the Virgin Mary) as models of holiness. And this is solidly biblical. While Saint Paul says, "Be imitators of God, as beloved children" (Eph 5:1), he also says things like "be imitators of me" (1 Cor 4:16) and "be imitators of me, as I am of Christ" (1 Cor 11:1). If looking to a sinful human man like Saint Paul as a model of holiness isn't blasphemy, why would it be blasphemous to look to a man like Saint Joseph, or even a "frail, human woman" like the Mother of God? On the contrary, one of the reasons the Letter to the Hebrews focuses so much on the witness of the saints is that we need to become "imitators of those who through faith and patience inherit the promises" (Heb 6:12).

It's a further mistake to think that we look at the saints as models of holiness because we think that they're divine. We look at them as models of holiness precisely because they *aren't* divine. For instance, Mary is the perfect model of what it is to have faith, and Jesus isn't. But that's not because Jesus is inferior to Mary. Rather, his divinity means that he didn't have (or need) the virtue of faith. After all, "faith is the assurance of things hoped for, the conviction of things not seen" (Heb 11:1), and there's nothing that Jesus doesn't see (see Jn 3:11–13; 8:38). Christ is the perfect Bridegroom, and Mary and the saints show us how the Church, the Bride of Christ, ought to respond to him.

But in looking at the saints, isn't there a danger that we'll take our eyes off Jesus Christ? The New Testament doesn't seem to think so. Hebrews 11 gives a long litany of the saints of the Old Testament who lived by faith, followed by these words of encouragement: "Therefore, since we are surrounded by so great a cloud of witnesses, let us also lay aside every weight, and sin which clings so closely, and let us run with perseverance the race that is set before us, looking to Jesus the pioneer and perfecter of our faith, who for the joy that was set before him endured the cross, despising the shame, and is seated at the right hand of the throne of God" (Heb 12:1–2).

In other words, the author of Hebrews seems to think that the witness of the saints will *help* us to keep our eyes fixed on Jesus, and that we'll be better able to "run with perseverance the race" if we do so knowing that we are surrounded by innumerable saints.

The imagery is of a runner in a race, casting off every encumbrance holding him back. And in this image, the saints are the cheering crowds in the stands. Readers who aren't big sports fans may miss the importance of this detail. There's a well-documented "home-field advantage," meaning that teams playing in their own stadiums (and in front of their own fans) are more likely to win than visiting teams. A crucial part of that advantage is the boost that comes from having fans in the stands roaring out their support. In fact, when COVID-19 forced professional soccer teams in Germany to switch from full to empty stadiums partway through the season, the home-team advantage actually turned into a home-team disadvantage.[2] All of this is to say that having a crowd cheering you on really does make a difference; you actually perform better. And that's the point that Hebrews is making: We have a supportive crowd cheering us on, and knowing that enables us to run the race better, with our eyes fixed on Jesus. We imitate the saints, just as they imitated Christ.

This point is true not only of morality, in knowing how to behave; it's also an important point in theology, in knowing what to believe. In the history of theological debates, the debates over Mary and the saints were really debates about Jesus. For instance, when Christians in the second century went to battle against the Gnostics (the first major heresy facing Christianity), they pointed to Mary's critical role in salvation history as part of their defense of the humanity of Christ.[3] Likewise, when the fifth-century heretic Nestorius demanded that we call Mary "Mother of Christ" (*Christokos*, "Christ-bearer") instead of "Mother of God" (*Theotokos*, "God-bearer"), that looked like a fight about Mary.[4] But it was really a fight about Jesus Christ, for if Mary is the Mother of Christ, but not the Mother of God, then Christ is not God.[5]

The *Catechism of the Catholic Church* (CCC) sums up this idea by saying that "what the Catholic faith believes about Mary is based on what it believes about Christ, and what it teaches about Mary illumines in turn its faith in Christ" (487). In the same way, a Christ-centered view of Mary helps us to understand Christ better. Much the same can be said for Saint Joseph. To make sense of Joseph, you need to understand both Jesus and Mary. And making sense of Saint Joseph will, in turn, help to illuminate the truth about Jesus and Mary.

THE CHURCH'S FIRST PROTECTOR

What does it look like, concretely, to understand the life of Saint Joseph in the light of Jesus and Mary? A good place to start is with the first papal title ever granted to Saint Joseph: Patron of the Universal Church. As we saw in the last chapter, Saint Joseph went from being a mostly overlooked saint to being the second-favorite saint for popes to cite in magisterial teaching, and this was an important turning point on that journey. At the First Vatican Council (1869–70), the superiors general of forty-three religious orders signed a petition (called a *postulate*) asking that this title be officially bestowed upon Saint Joseph.[6] The pope at the time, Blessed Pius IX, quickly agreed to their request.

On December 8, 1870, the Sacred Congregation of Rites[7] announced that the pope, "in order to entrust himself and all the faithful to the Patriarch Saint Joseph's most powerful patronage, has chosen to comply with the prelates' desire and has solemnly declared him Patron of the Catholic Church."[8] The decree was intentionally released on the feast of the Immaculate Conception, a "day sacred to the Immaculate Virgin Mother of God, the most chaste Joseph's Spouse."[9] When Pope Francis announced a Year of Saint Joseph in 2020, he likewise timed it to begin on December 8, 150 years to the day after the declaration of Joseph as Patron of the Universal Church.[10]

So what's the biblical basis for the idea of Joseph as the Patron of the Universal Church, and what does it have to do with Mary? To answer that, consider Mary's relationship to the Church, and Joseph's relationship to Mary. Steve Manskar, an elder in the United Methodist Church, has lamented that "Mary has been virtually ignored" and "pushed to the edges of the story of salvation" in his own faith tradition.[11] He offers three reasons to take Mary more seriously. First, she "plays a critical role in God's mission to save the world," as the one who carried Jesus in her womb and who "nursed, mothered and raised Jesus into the man who changed the world; the Savior and Lord of the universe."[12] Second, "Mary is the first disciple." She's the first to hear the message of the

Incarnation, and her faithful yes makes her the first Christian. Even when the Twelve fall away in fear (see Mt 26:56), Mary remains faithful, following Jesus even to the foot of the cross (Jn 19:25) and beyond (Acts 1:14).

But the early Christians realized that Mary isn't just the Church's prototype as the first disciple; she's also the Church's archetype as the model disciple.[13] As Manskar explains: "Mary is a model of the Church as the people of God who are called to be Christ-bearers in the world. Each baptized Christian is chosen and called by God to be like Mary. When we look at Mary we see that God wants Christ to grow and be seen in each of us. As Christ is born in your heart, you bear him in the world and offer him to others."[14]

The *Catechism* sums this up by saying that Mary is "the symbol and the most perfect realization of the Church" (507). In one sense, we can say that when Christ became Incarnate, the entire visible Church was Mary.[15] The Body of Christ, both in the literal sense of Jesus' body and the mystical sense of the Church (see Col 1:18; Eph 5:23), first appears within Mary. Saint Paul describes the "fullness" of Christ as Jesus the head united with his body, the Church (Eph 1:22–23), a union first accomplished in the womb of his mother. And Saint Joseph is entrusted with the protection of this union. In the words of Pope Leo XIII, "The divine house which Joseph ruled with the authority of a father, contained within its limits the scarce-born Church."[16]

It's fitting that the Church was first a family, because each family is called to be a "domestic church" in which parents (by both word and example) serve as "the first preachers of the faith to their children," helping them to discern where God is calling each of them.[17] As we'll see in greater detail in later chapters, the Holy Family was a true family, in the fullest sense of the word. Joseph and Mary really were husband and wife, and Joseph really was a father to the child Jesus. It's true that this family was unusual in many respects, but what family isn't? At times, our emphasis on what made the Holy Family unlike other families — for example, that Joseph wasn't the biological father of Jesus, or that the union between Joseph and Mary wasn't a sexual one — can cause us to overlook the reality of what their family and ours have in common. We mustn't lose sight of the plain, ordinary fact that God entered history through the family, because this fact shapes almost everything we know and believe about both the family and the Church. As the *Catechism* says: "Christ chose to be born and grow up in the bosom of the holy family of Joseph and Mary. The Church is nothing other than 'the family of God'" (1655).

It will take the course of this book to unpack the significance of God's decision to act in this way and what it tells us about Joseph, Mary, the Church, and ourselves. But for now, it's worth pointing out just one aspect: that Joseph was chosen to be the protector of Mary, Jesus, and (by extension) the whole Church. In one sense, Joseph is the obvious choice — after all, he's the father of the family. But in another sense, he's the least obvious choice within the family. We could easily imagine Jesus being the one to make all of the family decisions from day one. After all, the Magi refer to him as "he who has been born king of the Jews," and when they see the infant Jesus, they fall before him in worship (see Mt 2:2, 11). But Scripture describes the child Jesus as being obedient to Joseph and Mary (Lk 2:51). We could likewise imagine, given the special role God gave to Mary, that God would communicate everything to (and through) her. But again, that's not what Scripture says.

Instead, there are four times after the Annunciation when God sends an angelic message to someone in the Holy Family, and each time it's to Saint Joseph. God chooses to respect the structure of the family and the headship in which Joseph humbly and unworthily finds himself as husband, father, and protector of the family. Perhaps the clearest demonstration of God's supporting Joseph in his role as family protector is in the message that Joseph receives after the Magi depart: "Rise, take the child and his mother, and flee to Egypt, and remain there till I tell you; for Herod is about to search for the child, to destroy him" (Mt 2:13).

Perhaps we've heard this story so many times that it is no longer shocking. But God sent an angel to Joseph in order to communicate to him that the most powerful secular authority in the area, King Herod, was plotting to murder Joseph's adopted son. That Herod was capable of such brutality is beyond question. According to the Jewish historian Josephus, Herod was worried on his deathbed that the Jews would rejoice, rather than mourn, upon his passing. His proposed solution (which fortunately was thwarted) was to gather up "the principal men of the entire Jewish nation," accuse them of crimes, and have them executed, simply to ensure that he would "have a great mourning at his funeral, and such as never had any king before him."[18] But what's more, the child whom Herod sought to "destroy" was not just any infant, but the Jewish Messiah and the God of Israel in the flesh.

The timing of the angel's visit is also important. These days, it's taken almost for granted that "Christ Jesus came into the world to save sinners" (1 Tm 1:15) and that this salvation was achieved through the Cross. But the fact that the Messiah would suffer and die was shocking to the earliest Christians. Saint Peter actually "rebuked" Jesus for teaching that "he must go to Jerusalem and suffer many things from the elders and chief priests and scribes, and be killed, and on the third day be raised" (Mt 16:21). On Easter morning, we still find two disciples unsure of what to make of a dead Messiah and needing Jesus to explain to them how this was indeed taught by "Moses and all the prophets" (Lk 24:27). And we can see this shocking twist even in the gifts of the Magi.

The Old Testament had foretold that the "the kings of Sheba and Seba" would come bearing gifts for the Messiah, including "gold of Sheba," and how "all kings fall down before him, / all nations serve him" (Ps 72:10–11, 15). The imagery here is of royal tributes being paid to a king greater than all the kings on earth. The prophet Isaiah expands upon this image by telling of how "all those from Sheba shall come. They shall bring gold and frankincense" (Is 60:6), combining the image of the tribute given to a king (gold), and the tribute given to God (frankincense; see Lv 2:1–2). But when the Magi finally arrive, they come bearing not only gold and frankincense, but myrrh, a spice associated (among other things) with burial and which would later be used in Jesus' burial (Jn 19:39). Joseph, immediately after seeing the Christ child presented with gold, frankincense, and myrrh, is told that the king wants to destroy his child. The idea of the Messiah suffering and dying is no longer a question of theological speculation, but a real life-or-death situation facing the Holy Family.

And so Joseph protects his family by taking them in the middle of the night into Egypt. As we'll see in chapter 6, this required a tremendous amount of courage and creativity, as Joseph was forced to find a place to live, restart his business from the ground up, and take care of his family. He had no idea how long the family would be staying in Egypt. The Gospel tells us that Joseph "rose and took the child and his mother by night, and departed to Egypt" (Mt 2:14). It seems unlikely that the Holy Family had either the time or the means to take much of anything else, particularly given that their intent seems to have been to slip out under cover of darkness. In reading the infancy narratives, it's easy to skim through this part, paying little attention to what a difficult and frightening journey this must have been.

This is what it meant for Joseph to protect his domestic church: to be willing to give up everything he had for the good of Jesus, just as he had previously done by shielding Mary from false allegations of adultery (see Mt 1:19). In serving them, he was serving the entire Church, both then and now. When we, through our adoption as the children of God, become Christ's brothers (Mk 3:34; Rom 8:29; Heb 2:11), we are being grafted into the family that was entrusted to the care of Saint Joseph. As Pope Francis has said:

> The Son of the Almighty came into our world in a state of great vulnerability. He needed to be defended, protected, cared for and raised by Joseph. God trusted Joseph, as did Mary, who found in him someone who would not only save her life, but would always provide for her and her child. In this sense, Saint Joseph could not be other than the Guardian of the Church, for the Church is the continuation of the Body of Christ in history, even as Mary's motherhood is reflected in the motherhood of the Church.[19]

Particular saints are invoked as the patrons of particular causes, often something that they cared deeply about during their earthly lives. (For instance, Saint Thomas More, who was a lawyer, is the patron saint of lawyers.) But Saint Joseph is the patron saint entrusted with the whole Church, precisely because God entrusted him during his earthly life with the care of the whole Christ, head and body.

PRAYER

One of the ways in which Pope Leo XIII encouraged the Church's growing devotion to Saint Joseph was by sharing a prayer to Saint Joseph which he asked to be prayed "during the whole month of October, at the recitation of the Rosary."[20] The prayer fleshes out what it means, concretely, for Saint Joseph to be our patron:

> To thee, O blessed Joseph, we have recourse in our affliction, and having implored the help of thy thrice holy Spouse, we now, with hearts filled with confidence, earnestly beg thee also to take us under thy protection. By that charity wherewith thou wert united to the Immaculate Virgin Mother of God, and by that fatherly love with which thou didst cherish the Child Jesus, we beseech thee and we humbly pray that thou wilt look down with gracious eye upon that inheritance which Jesus Christ purchased by his blood, and wilt succor us in our need by thy power and strength.
>
> Defend, O most watchful guardian of the Holy Family, the chosen offspring of Jesus Christ. Keep from us, O most loving Father, all blight of error and corruption. Aid us from on high, most valiant defender, in this conflict with the powers of darkness. And even as of old thou didst rescue the Child Jesus from the peril of his life, so now defend God's Holy Church from the snares of the enemy and from all adversity. Shield us ever under thy patronage, that, following thine example and strengthened by thy help, we may live a holy life, die a happy death, and attain to everlasting bliss in heaven. Amen.

QUESTIONS

1. Why is it fitting that Joseph should be named the Patron of the Universal Church?

2. How important is it that Jesus entered the world through a family?

3. Do I think of my own family as a "domestic church"? Why or why not?

4. In 1937, Pope Pius XI placed "the vast campaign of the Church against world Communism under the standard of St. Joseph, her mighty Protector."[21] What are the problems in my life that I need to place under the protection of Saint Joseph?

5. Am I, like Joseph, truly willing to give up everything for Jesus? What are the things that I find hardest to let go of?

3.

The Most Chaste Spouse

It's time to get the Christmas story right. One of the reasons we misunderstand Saint Joseph is that we don't really understand the story of the Incarnation. The popular story sounds something like this: Before they were married, Saint Joseph discovered that the Virgin Mary was pregnant. Because he was an observer of the law, and because he assumed that Mary must be an adulteress, Joseph planned to divorce her; but to avoid exposing her to humiliation (or stoning), he decided to do so quietly. At this point in the story, an angel appeared to Joseph in a dream and explained that the child was actually the Son of God. Joseph got permission from the angel to "take Mary your wife," which is assumed to mean permission to marry her, or else a sexual euphemism. But Joseph would not have marital relations with Mary at first for some reason, so he "took his wife, but knew her not until she had borne a son" (Mt 1:24–25).

The trouble with this version of the story is that it gets nearly every detail wrong, or at least in a way that we don't really understand. Let's start with the most obvious: Was the Virgin Mary an unwed mother? And why should we care one way or the other?

WAS MARY AN UNWED MOTHER?

Larry Pickens, a prominent pastor in the United Methodist Church, has written that "the story of Jesus's birth represents the experience of a poor unwed mother and her mate searching for a place to have her baby in the midst of poverty and displacement."[1] This mischaracterization is not unique to Protestants. Marge Fenelon, in her book *Imitating Mary: Ten Marian Virtues for the Modern Mom*, devotes an entire chapter to "The Unwed Mother," in which she speculates that during the Visitation, Mary probably "wasn't eager to share with the other travelers that she was an unwed mother. She had to bear that burden alone. If anyone found out, she might have ended up being stoned to death rather than returning home to Joseph."[2] Even Sister Dede Byrne, in her speech at the 2020 Republican National Convention, said that, "as Christians, we first met Jesus as a stirring embryo in the womb of an unwed mother."[3]

These are not off-the-cuff remarks, but prepared statements by religious leaders and authors who try to make points about society today based on Mary's supposed unwed motherhood. And it's easy to see why so many think she was unwed. In many English translations of the Bible, Matthew 1:18, Luke 1:27, and Luke 2:5 say that Mary and Joseph were "betrothed" or even "engaged."[4] Some translations, such as the RSV and the RSVCE, even have Mary saying in response to news of the Incarnation, "How can this be, since I have no husband?" (Lk 1:34). But on closer examination, something is amiss. After all, in Matthew's parallel account, we hear that Mary's "husband Joseph, being a just man and unwilling to put her to shame, resolved to send her away quietly" (Mt 1:19). How can Matthew describe Joseph as Mary's husband if she has no husband? And why would Joseph be contemplating divorce (see Mt 19:7) if he had no wife?

More subtly, note that Joseph seems to think that if he divorces Mary quietly, he'll avoid putting her to shame. But it would hardly spare Mary any shame if Joseph were to suggest that her child was the product of their fornication rather than her adultery.[5] If Jesus *was* conceived out of wedlock, he would have been barred from entering the Temple under Mosaic Law (see Dt 23:2). Yet we see him regularly entering, and even teaching in, the Temple (Mk 14:49; Lk 21:37) and speaking of the Temple both as his Father's house (Lk 2:41–49) and even seemingly as "my house" (Mt 21:13). Imagine how eagerly the scribes and Pharisees would have responded that *no*, this wasn't his father's house, and since his father conceived him out of wedlock, it wasn't his house either. After all, in John 8:41, after Jesus tells the Pharisees that they aren't true sons of Abraham, they respond by suggesting that he's the one who is "born of fornication." The charge is obviously false, but it shows the level of shame involved with such an allegation. Other early opponents of Christianity tried to discredit Jesus by claiming that he was the illegitimate son of a Roman soldier.[6] But why concoct such a story if the truth was that he *was* illegitimate? After all, to call Mary an unwed mother is to call Jesus a bastard.

Indeed, the whole Nativity story makes little sense if Mary and Joseph aren't married. When we see Joseph and Mary, they were traveling together to go to his ancestral hometown to be enrolled in the census, and they were apparently planning on staying together in a local inn (see Lk 2:7). That's not the kind of behavior one would expect if they were just engaged. I don't just mean the eyebrow-raising detail of shared accommodations either: I mean that you don't list a girlfriend (or even a fiancée) on a census form.

JOSEPH AND MARY'S TWO-STAGE JEWISH WEDDING

So what's going on here? The answer is that Mary and Joseph *were* married, and that the only reason it seems as if they weren't is that we don't understand ancient Jewish wedding rituals, and don't have the vocabulary to describe them neatly in English. At that time, Jewish marriages happened in two phases. After all, there was nothing like a "bachelor pad" at the time.[7] A man typically lived with his parents until his wedding day. After the wedding, his bride would continue to live with her father while he spent the next year quite literally getting his house in order.[8] Once he had prepared a house for her, she would move in with him. The first phase of the wedding, in which the two were legally bound, was known as the *kiddushin*; the second phase was called the *nissuin*.[9]

Jesus refers to this two-phase wedding ritual at the Last Supper, when he promises: "In my Father's house are many rooms; if it were not so, would I have told you that I go to prepare a place for you? And when I go and prepare a place for you, I will come again and will take you to myself, that where I am you may be also" (Jn 14:2–3). In other words, the Church is already the Bride of Christ (see Eph 5:25–32; 2 Cor 11:2), meaning that the *kiddushin* has taken place. But we don't yet live with our Bridegroom (Lk 5:34–35). We wait in eager anticipation for Christ to take us to our new home to be with him forever. That's the meaning of the *nissuin* ritual, and it's what is foretold in the great heavenly wedding feast in Revelation 19:6–10.

There's another important detail to note here, to make sense of the wedding of Joseph and Mary (although I'll warn you: It's going to make things more confusing before it makes them clearer). During the first century, marital sex was permitted between the time of the *kiddushin* and the *nissuin*.[10] In fact, the ancient Jewish commentary (called a *Mishna*) on the *kiddushin* said that a wife "is acquired by money, by deed, or by intercourse."[11] If an unmarried man and woman, with the intent to marry, slept with one another, that was considered a valid way of contracting the *kiddushin*.[12] Although this mode of *kiddushin* would fall out of favor with later rabbis,[13] it was accepted as valid in ancient Judaism; in fact, it appears to be how Abraham's son Isaac became married to Rebekah in the days before the Temple (see Gn 24:67). And since sexual relations were a biblically and rabbinically accepted way of bringing about the *kiddushin*, it of course follows that there was no scandal attached to sexual relations (or pregnancy) after the *kiddushin*.[14] This explains why, so long as people assumed that Saint Joseph was Jesus' father, there was no whiff of scandal.[15]

Understanding this should radically change how we understand the Christmas story. Mary *doesn't* say to the angel, "How can this be, since I have no husband?" She actually says, "How can this be, since I know not a man?" (*Pōs estai touto epei andra ou ginōskō?*) The "knowing" (*ginōskō*) was a Jewish sexual euphemism (see Gn 4:1, 17). In other words, Mary isn't saying that she's unmarried. She's saying that she's a virgin. And this is a very odd thing for her to say. As we've just seen, Mary and Joseph were allowed to have sexual relations, since they were already married at this point. And yet Mary is saying to the angel that she *isn't* having sexual relations with Joseph. Indeed, her question even seems to imply that she's not planning to, either. Otherwise, how can we make sense of her confusion at the idea of having a son?

But the biblical account is going to become stranger. Saint Matthew tells us how, after Saint Joseph rose from the dream in which an angel visited him, "he took his wife, but knew her not until she had borne a son" (Mt 1:24–25). A lot of attention has been paid to the meaning of that word *until*. John MacArthur, for instance, writes that "Matthew makes it clear that she remained a virgin until she gave birth, implying that normal marital relations began after that time," as if Matthew's goal (like MacArthur's) was to refute Catholic belief in the perpetual virginity of Mary, or as if Matthew were trying to explain the birds and bees to his readers.[16] Such a reading totally ignores the context of Matthew's Gospel and Matthew's explanation of why he is including the details that he includes.

If you say to your children, "Be good until I return," you're not asking them to misbehave upon your return. Rather, your *until* is marking off a certain period of time during which you're particularly concerned about their good behavior. Likewise, when Matthew says that Joseph and Mary did not have sex *until* the birth of Jesus, he's not trying to tell us that they had sex on or after Christmas. He's marking off a period of time in which he's particularly interested in Mary's virginity — namely, from Jesus' conception to his birth. And why does he care about that? He tells us explicitly: Because this means that both halves of the Messianic prophecy in Isaiah 7:14, that a virgin "shall conceive *and bear* a son," have been fulfilled (see Mt 1:22–23).[17] Those who argue against Mary's perpetual virginity on the basis of Matthew 1:25 are taking the verse wildly out of context to try to force Matthew into say something that he isn't.

THE VIRGINAL CONSUMMATION

Unfortunately, our obsession with that *until* has caused us to overlook a much stranger aspect of Matthew 1:24. When Matthew says that Joseph "took his wife," that's not a sexual euphemism in the way that "knowing her" would be. Taking his wife is a reference to the *nissuin*: Matthew is telling us that, rather than divorcing Mary, Joseph rose from the dream and proceeded with the second stage of the wedding by bringing her into his home. At this point, Mary and Joseph were married and living together, and — at least for the duration of her pregnancy — were still not having sex. In other words, what's remarkable enough to make it into Scripture isn't the idea that a married couple might be sleeping with each other. It's that this married couple *isn't*. Once more, we should be asking: What is going on here?

Protestant commentators tend to have no good explanation for this confusing detail. For instance, one biblical commentary says that "there is no explanation as to why Joseph abstained from physical intimacy with his wife until Jesus was born in Bethlehem of Judea. (Some think Joseph had been instructed by an angel to do so.)"[18] But Matthew has just recounted the details of the angel's words to Joseph (see Mt 1:20–21) and made no mention of any such instructions. Are we to assume that the evangelist failed to include the very part of the conversation that would be needed to make sense of what happened next? Additionally, Joseph's dream seems to have happened at some point after the angel Gabriel visited Mary. Are we to assume that the angels were simply hoping that the couple would abstain until then?

The evangelical Charles "Chuck" Swindoll suggests a second theory: that it speaks to how "honorable and righteous" Saint Joseph was that "he kept Mary sexually pure through the birth of the Messiah," despite all the "whispered rumors" about "Mary's premarital infidelity or about Joseph's inability to keep himself pure prior to the consummation of their wedding."[19] As we've seen, this badly misunderstands the marital relationship between Joseph and Mary. There would be no "whispered rumors," and Swindoll's account (by itself) doesn't explain why it is honorable or righteous to keep one's wife "sexually pure" by not engaging in marital relations.

In other words, we seem to be left with a mystery. On the one hand, it's clear from Matthew 1:23 that for the Virgin Birth prophecy of Isaiah 7:14 to be fulfilled, Mary must be a virgin both at the Annunciation and nine months later, at Christmas. But there's no indication that either the angel Gabriel or the angel who visited Saint Joseph found it necessary to give either spouse any kind of instruction to refrain from having sexual relations. On the contrary, it's Mary who brings up the issue of sexual abstinence. Having been told that she's about to bear the Savior of the World, the part that she seems to find most confusing is that she's going to bear a child. The strong implication, never spelled out, is that she and Joseph were never planning on having sex, and that this accounts for why the angels didn't need to provide any instructions. For those who reject the perpetual virginity of Mary (dogmatically defined by the Council of Ephesus as far back as 431), it seems impossible to make any kind of sense of the Christmas story. Fortunately, there is a better way.

THE VIRGIN MOTHER AND
THE MOST CHASTE SPOUSE

So far, we've talked a lot about what the marriage between Joseph and Mary *wasn't*, and all of the ways that our culture (and even some of our religious leaders) get the story wrong in big ways. But what *was* it like?

To make any sense of their marriage, we first need to purify purity of some of its erroneous connotations. The word purity has two related senses: "clean" and "unmixed."[20] These two meanings often overlap, but they don't mean the same thing. We can say that something is "pure evil," for instance, and we plainly mean only the second of these two. It's important to recognize this, because we hear a lot of talk about "virginal purity," and it's easy to conclude from this that virginity is clean and sex is dirty. But while there is a sense in which virginity is freedom from the corruption of lust, there's also a sense in which Christian virginity is about being "unmixed," of being dedicated wholly to God. Holiness, in the original sense, refers to the state of being "set apart" for God.[21] And Saint Paul speaks about how those dedicated to a life of virginity are uniquely capable of living out this kind of holiness: "The unmarried man is anxious about the affairs of the Lord, how to please the Lord; but the married man is anxious about worldly affairs, how to please his wife, and his interests are divided. And the unmarried woman or virgin is anxious about the affairs of the Lord, how to be holy in body and spirit; but the married woman is anxious about worldly affairs, how to please her husband" (1 Cor 7:32–34).

In other words, the issue is not that marriage and sex are bad. They are gifts from God. But there are some who are called to forgo these goods for an even greater good: single-minded devotion to God. Jesus speaks of those who receive this calling as "eunuchs for the sake of the kingdom of heaven" (Mt 19:12). They are called, in other words, to be purely and exclusively dedicated to God. It's clear from both the words of Jesus and the writings of Saint Paul that this holy virginity has always been understood as the highest state in the Christian life. Jesus concludes his teaching on celibacy with an invitation: "He who is able to receive this, let him receive it" (Mt 19:12). Saint Paul likewise says,

"I wish that all were as I myself am," while acknowledging that "each has his own special gift from God," and that if the unmarried "cannot exercise self-control, they should marry. For it is better to marry than to be aflame with passion" (1 Cor 7:7, 9).

The third commandment says to keep the Sabbath "holy" (Ex 20:8). That doesn't mean that the other days of the week are evil or that God is less present to you on those other days. It means simply that your mind is divided the rest of the week, as you try to encounter God in the workaday world, and you have one day a week set aside to focus exclusively on him. What the Sabbath is to the week, celibates are to the Christian community. That's the meaning of holy virginity.[22]

This is at the heart of the paradox of the Virgin Birth. Mary is at once called to this highest state of celibacy *and* called to the good of marriage and motherhood. In any other family, the worldly concerns of your children risk taking your mind off God. In this family, the worldly concerns of her child were the concerns of God. There was no potential conflict between her maternal love for her son and her service of God. No one else on earth has ever experienced this — no one, that is, but Saint Joseph. Saint John Paul II writes that Saint Joseph "shared" in the Incarnation "like no other human being except Mary, the Mother of the Incarnate Word," and that he shared in it with her because "he was involved in the same salvific event."[23]

And this is why it is so important that this dual calling to virginity and family life is one that the couple freely chose. In the words of Saint Augustine, Mary's "virginity also itself was on this account more pleasing and accepted, in that it was not that Christ being conceived in her, rescued it beforehand from a husband who would have violated it, Himself to preserve it; but, before he was conceived, chose it, already dedicated to God, as that from which to be born."[24] In other words, Mary didn't have virginity forced upon her by the angel Gabriel. She *desired* the highest level of single-minded devotion to God.

The idea that Mary seems to have made some kind of vow of virginity prior to the Annunciation isn't just some weird idea dreamed up by noncanonical writings such as the Protoevangelium of James.[25] In fact, it seems to be implicit within Saint Luke's infancy narrative. Saint Augustine argues that Mary's question to the angel Gabriel makes no sense "unless she had before vowed herself unto God as a virgin."[26] In other words, Mary wasn't confused about the birds and the bees. She was trying to understand what to make of the vow of virginity that she had apparently made in the face of the news that she (still a virgin) was going to be a mother. Was God asking her to leave aside this vow for the sake of some greater good? No, the angel explains: "The Holy Spirit will come upon you, / and the power of the Most High will overshadow you; / therefore the child to be born will be called holy, / the Son of God" (Lk 1:35). There it is again: that interconnected discussion of virginity and holiness. What's missing in the Protestant readings of the infancy narratives is that the angel Gabriel appears to be reassuring Mary that she's not going to lose her virginity. (This would be particularly odd if she was planning to lose her virginity nine months later.)

So what is Saint Joseph's role in all of this? According to Augustine, it was to protect Mary's virginity and to "guard against violent persons, what she had already vowed."[27] In other words, Joseph is called to be the "most chaste spouse" of Mary, a calling only a bit less paradoxical than Mary's. He's called to be her true husband, but in a manner ordered toward the maintenance of her virginity.

THE TRUE MARRIAGE
OF JOSEPH AND MARY

In the early Christian folk stories, Saint Joseph is thrust into this role, more or less against his will.[28] More likely, Saint Joseph chose to do this, offering himself in marriage to help Mary to live out her promise of perpetual virginity. Women in the ancient world — and particularly widows, virgins, and the unmarried — were in a precarious social and economic position. We see in Jesus a special concern for such women. When he passed the body of a dead man who was "the only son of his mother, and she was a widow," we're told that "when the Lord saw her, he had compassion on her" and raised her son back to life and "gave him to his mother" (see Lk 7:12–15). The point of the story isn't that Christ had compassion on the dead man, but that he recognized the awful situation that the man's death left his mother in, and so he miraculously intervened. Likewise, when Jesus' own mother was mourning the dying of her only son, he looked out for her from the cross by entrusting her to the care of the apostle John (Jn 19:26–27), strong evidence that Jesus' so-called brothers and sisters weren't literally Mary's children. This is the Christian model, the "pure and undefiled" religion that Saint James speaks of: "to visit orphans and widows in their affliction, and to keep oneself unstained from the world" (Jas 1:27). Perhaps it's only right that Joseph, the "just man" (Mt 1:19), lived out this pure religion, softening the "affliction" that Mary's virginity created, without staining himself with worldliness.

But in recognizing this as holy and religious, we shouldn't miss that there's also something manly about it. The Christian vision of strength is captured by Saint Paul, who says that "we who are strong ought to bear with the failings of the weak, and not to please ourselves" (Rom 15:1). The modern world likes to pretend that men and women are not only equal, but even interchangeable. We pretend — in spite of all the evidence — that men and women are the same and that we're equally good at everything. And when the world does acknowledge that manly strength exists, it often demonizes it as "privilege" or "toxic masculinity." But the Christian message is a radically different one: Men, you are strong (often, strong in ways that the world can't even see), and this strength is a gift from God, not for you to dominate others or achieve self-gratification, but for you to show Christ to the world by serving those around you who are weaker.

Of course, this isn't true only of men, but there are ways in which men are uniquely equipped and called to show this kind of strength of service. Saint Peter expresses it simply, telling husbands to "live considerately with your wives, bestowing honor on the woman as the weaker sex, since you are joint heirs of the grace of life, in order that your prayers may not be hindered" (1 Pt 3:7). He doesn't say, "You're stronger than your wife, so you're better." He says, "You're stronger than your wife, but she's your equal, your coheir of eternal life, so if you want to grow spiritually, you need to bestow honor upon her." Men and women tend to be strong in different ways. By making men the stronger of the two sexes in particular aspects of life, God was not expressing a preference for masculinity over femininity; rather, he was entrusting men with a sacred duty, one that we see both Jesus and Saint Joseph living out in a radical way.

If this theory is correct, then Joseph's act of sacrifice is almost as incredible as Mary's. She offers up her femininity to God, and he offers his masculinity to her to aid her in her offering. Their marriage is sexed, but not sexual — that is, it isn't some denuded sham of a marriage. He offers her himself and his body, not in the sexual act, but in the act of preserving her virginity. Archbishop Fulton Sheen was right to criticize depictions of Saint Joseph as an old man (in art and literature), which have "unconsciously made Joseph a spouse chaste and pure by age rather than virtue."[29] Instead, Joseph "was probably a young man, strong, virile, athletic, handsome, chaste, and disciplined; the kind of man one sees sometimes shepherding sheep, or piloting a plane, or working at a carpenter's bench. Instead of being a man incapable of love, he must have been on fire with love."[30] And this virile young man, on fire with love (rather than aflame with lust), used his manliness to care for his family, to earn a living through manual labor, and to keep his wife and son safe from all physical and spiritual dangers.

When medieval Christians read Song of Solomon 4:12 ("a garden locked is my sister, my bride, / a garden locked, a fountain sealed"), they saw in this mystical image of the enclosed garden an image of the soul, of the Church, and of the Virgin Mary. The meaning is clearer if you know that the Greek name for a walled garden is *paradeisos*, the root of our word paradise. One can scarcely hear of "the garden" or *paradeisos* without recalling the Garden of Eden. But it's also a reminder that, after the Fall, this paradise needs protecting. God "drove out the man; and at the east of the garden of Eden he placed the cherubim, and a flaming sword which turned every way, to guard the way to the tree of life" (Gn 3:24). The role of Saint Joseph is that of the cherub with the flaming sword, guarding the new "enclosed garden," within which the Tree of Life has begun to grow. He is called to offer his strength in the service of holiness and purity.

THE CHASTE MARRIAGE

The marriage of Joseph and Mary was not only a true marriage, but a model for marriage. Indeed, it helped to redeem the idea of marriage, which had been corrupted by the dual influences of paganism and sinfulness. God warned Eve that, on account of the Fall, "your desire shall be for your husband, / and he shall rule over you" (Gn 3:16), and this is the story of much of human history. As Saint Jerome explained, "Earthly laws give a free rein to the unchastity of men, merely condemning seduction and adultery; lust is allowed to range unrestrained among brothels and slave girls, as if the guilt were constituted by the rank of the person assailed and not by the purpose of the assailant."[31]

Both Christians and non-Christians have sometimes acted as if Christian marriage were simply a means by which to "be fruitful and multiply."[32] But this is precisely what early Christians rejected in their embrace of a Christian view of marriage. In the pagan world, as Pope Leo XIII observed, "nothing could be more piteous than the wife, sunk so low as to be all but reckoned as a means for the gratification of passion, or for the production of offspring."[33] It was Christianity that challenged this, calling men to live as chastely as the world had long demanded of women: for "with us Christians what is unlawful for women is equally unlawful for men, and as both serve the same God both are bound by the same obligations."[34]

In other words, it's not just Mary who was called to chastity. It was indispensable that Joseph live this out as well. Chastity, it's worth noting here, isn't the same thing as virginity or celibacy. In the strict sense, chastity means "the successful integration of sexuality within the person and thus the inner unity of man in his bodily and spiritual being" (CCC 2337), and it's something to which all of us are called. It is easy to mistake sexual licentiousness for freedom and even strength; this was true in the ancient world and remains true today. But the radical message of Christianity is that true freedom and true strength are found not in sexual conquests, but in conquering one's own passions with the help of God, "that each one of you know how to control his own body in holiness and honor, not in the passion of lust like heathens who do not know God" (1 Thes 4:4–5).

But there's a broader way in which we can speak of chastity as well. The word chastity comes from the Latin word *castus*, from which we also get the words castigate and chastise. As Saint Thomas Aquinas explains, chastity "takes its name from the fact that reason 'chastises' concupiscence, which, like a child, needs curbing."[35] That's why Saint Augustine speaks of a sort of "chastity of the mind," in which we chasten our mind to love God and neighbor, rather than worldly pleasures.[36] And it's why Pope Francis can speak of chastity as a sort of "freedom from possessiveness in every sphere of one's life."[37] As the pope explains:

> Only when love is chaste, is it truly love. A possessive love ultimately becomes dangerous: it imprisons, constricts and makes for misery. God himself loved humanity with a chaste love; he left us free even to go astray and set ourselves against him. The logic of love is always the logic of freedom, and Joseph knew how to love with extraordinary freedom. He never made himself the center of things. He did not think of himself, but focused instead on the lives of Mary and Jesus.[38]

This much seems clear from the few words in Scripture about Saint Joseph. He does not appear as a man obsessed with his rights as a husband, or with his rights as a citizen to live undisturbed (being forced to leave his home first for the census, and then to avoid a murderous king), or in any other way insisting on putting himself first.

There's a beautiful parallel between Joseph's yes to God and the yes of his wife. When the angel Gabriel visited Mary, he concluded by saying, "Behold, your kinswoman Elizabeth in her old age has also conceived a son; and this is the sixth month with her who was called barren. For with God nothing will be impossible" (Lk 1:36–37). A person might be forgiven for taking a few moments after such an event to process what has just happened. Not so with Mary. Springing into action, she "arose and went with haste into the hill country, to a city of Judah" to take care of her pregnant kinswoman for three months (see Lk 1:39, 56). In service of others, she allowed her own life to be uprooted and her plans to be altered, with only a moment's notice. Her husband, after receiving word that Herod intended to kill them, did the same thing. Upon waking from the dream in which the angel had spoken to him, "he rose and took the child and his mother by night, and departed to Egypt" (Mt 2:14). Perhaps we want to give him only partial credit — after all, men were coming to kill the baby, so there was no time to waste! But we see this same promptness in his response to God even when it was not an emergency, as when an angel announced that Herod was dead and that it was time to go home (Mt 2:19–21).

Both Mary and Joseph hear the word of God and rise and go. This is the heart of chastity: to ask not "what can I get from the other?" but "what can I give?" And it is only in this way that we can experience true human freedom. As the Second Vatican Council says, "Man, who is the only creature on earth which God willed for itself, cannot fully find himself except through a sincere gift of himself."[39]

PRAYER

Saint John Henry Newman (1801–90) composed a beautiful *triduo* for Saint Joseph: a three-day prayer focused on the the "Glorious Titles of St. Joseph."[40] Here are the prayers for Day One, which seem particularly appropriate for this chapter, since the title on which it focuses is "Spouse of Mary":

> He was the true and worthy Spouse of Mary, supplying in a visible manner the place of Mary's Invisible Spouse, the Holy Ghost. He was a virgin, and his virginity was the faithful mirror of the virginity of Mary. He was the Cherub, placed to guard the new terrestrial Paradise from the intrusion of every foe.

> V. Blessed be the name of Joseph.
> R. Henceforth and forever. Amen.

> Let us pray.

> God, who in thine ineffable Providence didst vouchsafe to choose Blessed Joseph to be the husband of thy most holy Mother, grant, we beseech thee, that we may be made worthy to receive him for our intercessor in heaven, whom on earth we venerate as our holy Protector: who livest and reignest world without end. Amen.

QUESTIONS

1. Prior to reading this, did I think of Mary and Joseph as "engaged" at the Annunciation, or did I think of Mary as an unwed mother? How does understanding the Jewish context change how I read these New Testament accounts?

2. What does it mean to say that the marriage of Joseph and Mary was "sexed, but not sexual"? In what ways was Joseph a true spouse to Mary?

3. Why does it matter that Mary was a virgin?

4. In what way is Mary like the Sabbath? In what way is Joseph like the cherub holding the flaming sword?

5. Pope Leo XIII wrote that spouses find in Joseph "a perfect example of love, of peace, and of conjugal fidelity" while "virgins at the same time find in him the model and protector of virginal integrity."[41] In what way is Saint Joseph a model for my state in life?

6. What are concrete ways in which I can imitate the "freedom from possessiveness" that Joseph models within his marriage?

4.

Joseph the Just

In the previous chapter, we saw that many of our under-standings and assumptions about the Christmas story — and about the relationship between Joseph and Mary — are wrong. But there's one more widespread assumption that is worth addressing in depth: why Joseph contemplated divorcing Mary.

The ordinary view Christians today take upon reading the story is to assume that Joseph was suspicious of Mary, believing her to be an adulteress. And, indeed, plenty of early Christians read the story this way as well. But Saint Thomas Aquinas suggests that most of us are missing the meaning of the text here:

According to Jerome and Origen, [Joseph] did not

suspect adultery; for Joseph knew Mary's chastity; he read in Scripture that a virgin would conceive: "And there shall come forth a rod (*virga*) out of the root of Jesse, and a flower shall rise up out of his root," etc. (Isaiah 7:14; 11:1). He also knew that Mary had descended of the line of David. Hence, he more easily believed this to be fulfilled in her, than for her to have been ravished.[1]

But if Joseph suspected the Virgin Birth rather than adultery, why did he contemplate divorce? Because "considering himself to be unworthy to dwell with one of so great holiness, he wanted to put her away privately."[2] Needless to say, this would be a radically different way of understanding the story. So how can we tell which view is the correct one?

FOUR INITIAL REASONS TO RECONSIDER

To begin with, do we have any reason to second-guess the general assumption that Joseph suspected the Virgin Mary? We do — in fact, we have several. I would like to investigate four in particular. The first is simply that Joseph knew Mary much better than we do. Look at the portrait of Mary painted in the Scriptures and ask yourself if the woman described there seems likely to end up an adulteress. Joseph, although not privy to the details about what God had in store for her, would still have known the strength of her character and the fervor of her faith.

The second reason is related to the first: Joseph and Mary were both extremely holy. It's easy to imagine that the Incarnation sort of happened to them by chance, like winning a divine lottery. But God planned the Incarnation from all eternity, and out of all of the possible candidates he chose for Jesus to enter history through this couple. That already should tell us that there's something special about the two of them — an idea that will be reinforced by the biblical depiction of Mary as the Ark of the New Covenant, which we will explore in the next section. For now, suffice it to say that it's no exaggeration to describe both God and Israel as obsessed with the purity and holiness of the Ark, and that Mary seems to have fit this description of being pure and holy.

Third, Joseph is described as "being a just man and unwilling to put her to shame" (Mt 1:19). But Joseph wouldn't be "just" for rashly assuming that Mary's pregnancy was the result of adultery. Rather, "if one gives answer before he hears, / it is his folly and shame" (Prv 18:13). Even excluding the explanation of the Virgin Birth, how would he know (without asking) that she was an adulteress and not a victim? And as Saint Thomas Aquinas points out, if Joseph did suspect Mary of adultery, "how was he just if he was not willing to expose, that is, to make public, the crime of her whom he was suspecting of adultery?"[3] Covering up a crime (if that's what he thought he was doing) would scarcely fit the Jewish understanding of "a just man."

Some modern Protestants have recognized this but resolved the difficulty in the wrong direction. For instance, Bill Mounce, one of the translators of the NIV and ESV Bibles, asks, "Would a person characterized as 'just' ignore what appeared to be the fact that Mary had been sexually active during their engagement?" But rather than cause him to reconsider his view of Joseph's suspicions, Mounce instead concludes that the NIV was right to translate the verse as "Joseph her husband was faithful to the law, and yet (*ōn kai*) did not want to expose her to public disgrace."[4] The problem with this reading is that it views Joseph as a good man in spite of his faithfulness to God's law, not because of it, as if Joseph would have been a better man if he were more willing to disregard God's commandments.

Fourth, the Virgin Birth was a reasonable expectation. A number of Old Testament prophecies had pointed forward to the particular time and place in which the Jews of the first century found themselves. As a result, the people were searching eagerly for signs of the Messiah. When the Sanhedrin debated what to do with the followers of Christ, Gamaliel referenced two recent failed messianic movements (see Acts 5:34–37). Even Saint John the Baptist was suspected of being the Messiah: "The people were in expectation, and all men questioned in their hearts concerning John, whether perhaps he were the Christ" (Lk 3:15).

One of the hallmarks of a righteous man was this longing for the Messiah (see Mt 13:17), and Joseph would have been no exception in this regard.[5] One of these messianic prophecies had foretold that a virgin would conceive and bear a son (Is 7:14), which may be why one of the original arguments *against* Jesus was that "we know where this man comes from; and when the Christ appears, no one will know where he comes from" (Jn 7:27). In other words, keeping an eye out for the Messiah also meant keeping an eye out for a virgin conceiving and bearing a son. In that time and place, when that virgin (of the line of David!) announces that she's pregnant, Joseph has reason to think that something unusual is happening.

ARK OF THE NEW COVENANT

There's an additional reason to believe that Joseph had a better idea of what was going on than we typically give him credit for. After the Annunciation, Mary was almost immediately recognized by her kinswoman Saint Elizabeth as the

Ark of the New Covenant. The problem is, we Christians are often too ignorant of the Old Testament to understand this point. So perhaps a bit of background is in order.

It's not an exaggeration to say that the center of Israel's worship in the Old Testament was the Ark of the Covenant. It might be tempting to say that the center of worship was the Temple, but the Temple itself was built, as King David explained, to be "a house of rest for the ark of the covenant of the LORD" (1 Chr 28:2). Unable to build the Temple himself, David put the Ark in a tent and appointed "certain of the Levites as ministers before the ark of the LORD, to invoke, to thank, and to praise the LORD, the God of Israel," along with priests who were "to blow trumpets continually, before the ark of the covenant of God" (1 Chr 16:4, 6).

What made the Ark so important was that it was where the glory of the Lord was made manifest. In their war against the Philistines, the elders of Israel decided to "bring the ark of the covenant of the LORD here from Shiloh, that he may come among us and save us from the power of our enemies" (1 Sm 4:3). When the Ark was brought into the Israelite camp, the Philistines were afraid, saying, "A god has come into the camp" (1 Sm 4:7). In the ensuing battle, the Philistines captured the Ark and killed the attending priests (see 1 Sm 4:11). The pregnant widow of one of the priests named her son Ichabod (The Glory Is Not), saying, "The glory has departed from Israel!" (1 Sm 4:21). For their part, the Philistines understood themselves to have captured one of the many gods. But this god was a mighty one, and when the Ark was placed before the idol Dagon, the idol was destroyed, and the people were afflicted with tumors (1 Sm 5:1–10). Eventually, the terrified Philistines returned the Ark, "that it may not slay us and our people" (1 Sm 5:11).

With this background, we can see what an important

political and religious move it was for King David to decide
to move the Ark to his new capital, Jerusalem. We learn in
2 Samuel 6 that David "arose and went with all the people who were with him." They began their journey in the
hill country of Judah, in the town of Baale-judah, in "the
house of Abinadab which was on the hill" (vv. 2, 3). The ini-
tial attempt to move the Ark faltered when one of the oxen
slipped. One of the men, Uzzah, reached out and touched
the Ark and was struck dead on the spot (vv. 6–7). This
caused David to ask, "How can the ark of the LORD come to
me?" (v. 9). While David tried to plan his next move, "the
ark of the LORD remained in the house of Obed-edom the
Gittite three months; and the Lord blessed Obed-edom and
all his household" (v. 11). David took this blessing as a sign
of divine favor to continue the journey, and so he "brought
up the ark of God from the house of Obed-edom to the city
of David with rejoicing," and he "danced before the LORD
with all his might" (vv. 12, 14). In this way, God allowed the
center of worship, the Ark of the Covenant, to enter the city
of David, Jerusalem. When we speak of Jerusalem as "the
holy city" (Is 52:1 and Mt 4:5 are examples), it's because of
this. Without the Ark, there's no Temple; without the Temple, there's no "holy city."

If the Ark is the place where God dwells in his glory,
then Mary is the Ark of the New Covenant. That's not just
theological musing, either. Saint Luke takes pains to make
this connection. Immediately after hearing that God will
dwell in her womb, we're told that Mary "arose and went
with haste into the hill country, to a city of Judah" (Lk 1:39)
,to the house of Zechariah and Elizabeth. Nowhere else in
the New Testament do we find the phrase "arose and went,"
and it's no coincidence that Luke's account begins in this way.
Once more, we find ourselves in the hill country of Judah,

and the parallels don't stop there. Echoing David's question, "How can the ark of the LORD come to me?," Elizabeth asks, upon seeing Mary, "Why is this granted me, that the mother of my Lord should come to me?" (Lk 1:43). And how did Elizabeth know that she was the recipient of so great a blessing? Because "when the voice of your greeting came to my ears, the child in my womb leaped for joy" (Lk 1:44). Thus it fell to the unborn John the Baptist to fulfill the role once played by King David of dancing before the Ark and the glory of the Lord. Given all of the other parallels, it is hardly a shock when we then read that "Mary remained with her about three months" (Lk 1:56).

It's remarkable that Elizabeth recognized Mary as pregnant at all, given that Mary arose and went to see her immediately after the Annunciation. But she does, and her mind doesn't seem even for a moment to question whether Mary might be an adulteress, or even whether Mary's husband might be the father of her child. By the time the sound waves hit her ears, and her child stirs in her womb, she knows the truth. Of course, this tells us a great deal about Elizabeth's holiness and attentiveness to the voice of God, but it also tells us about the holiness of Mary, and of just how thick the messianic expectation must have hung in the air.

SAINT JOSEPH AND THE NUMINOUS

There's one final reason to suspect that Aquinas is correct in reading Saint Joseph's response to Mary as an expression of piety rather than suspicion: The very strange message that the angel brings to Joseph in the dream.

There's a popular myth that the phrase "be not afraid" or "fear not" appears exactly 365 times in the Bible, once for each day. The claim often sounds something like this: "There are 365 messages from God in the Bible that begin with a phrase like, 'Fear not!' In other words, every single day of the year, you can read a message from God that says, in effect, 'You don't need to be afraid. I am for you! I am with you! I love you!'"[6]

The twofold problem with this is that (1) it's not true,[7] and (2) it's missing some important context. We find the phrase "do not be afraid" eight times in the New Testament, and it's never in the context of Jesus' encouraging his discouraged followers. Rather, in each case, the phrase is used when someone is witnessing some shocking divine revelation. For example:

- When the angel Gabriel suddenly appears to Zechariah in the Temple (see Lk 1:13) and to the Virgin Mary (Lk 1:30)
- After Jesus performs the first miraculous catch of fish, and Peter and the other disciples are "astonished" (Lk 5:9–10)
- When the apostles see Jesus walking on the water and are "frightened" (Jn 6:19–20)
- When the Lord — and later, an angel — appears to Saint Paul in a dream (Acts 18:9; 27:23–24)
- When the women on Easter morning encounter an angel in the empty tomb (Mt 28:5) and then the Risen Christ (Mt 28:10)

In none of these cases do we find God cheering people up by reminding them that he is "for them." That message can be found in the New Testament, but not here. Rather, these texts are universally about calming down people who have just seen something truly awesome: the kind of transcendent religious experience that theologians call "numinous."[8]

C. S. Lewis illustrates the concept of the numinous this way:

Suppose you were told there was a tiger in the next room: you would know that you were in danger and would probably feel fear. But if you were told "There is a ghost in the next room," and believed it, you would feel, indeed, what is often called fear, but of a different kind. It would not be based on the knowledge of danger, for no one is primarily afraid of what a ghost may do to him, but of the mere fact that it is a ghost. It is "uncanny" rather than dangerous, and the special kind of fear it excites may be called Dread. With the Uncanny one has reached the fringes of the Numinous. Now suppose that you were told simply "There is a mighty spirit in the room," and believed it. Your feelings would then be even less like the mere fear of danger: but the disturbance would be profound. You would feel wonder and a certain shrinking — a sense of inadequacy to cope with such a visitant and of prostration before it — an emotion which might be expressed in Shakespeare's words "Under it my genius is rebuked." This feeling may be described as awe, and the object which excites it as the Numinous.[9]

For a clear example of the kind of awed fear inspired by the numinous, look at the reaction that Jacob had after awakening from the famous dream in which God revealed himself, and in which Jacob had a vision of angels ascending and descending on a sort of ladder between heaven and earth. When Jacob awoke, "he was afraid, and said, 'How awesome is this place! This is none other than the house of God, and this is the gate of heaven'" (Gn 28:17). Jacob named the spot Bethel, meaning "the house of God."

What does all of this have to do with Saint Joseph? As

Joseph was contemplating divorcing Mary, an angel appeared to him in a dream and said, "Joseph, son of David, do not fear to take Mary your wife, for that which is conceived in her is of the Holy Spirit; she will bear a son, and you shall call his name Jesus, for he will save his people from their sins" (Mt 1:20–21). The thing that's strange about this is that, given that an angel is appearing to Joseph in a dream, we might expect to hear a "do not fear" to calm Joseph's awed fear of the angel. But instead, the angel is calming Joseph's awed fear of *taking Mary as his wife.*

Connecting the dots, it makes perfect sense that a pious Jew like Joseph would be properly terrified of Mary. Her womb is the new Bethel, the new house of God. And she is the new Ark of the Covenant. Elizabeth recognized it in an instant. If Joseph recognized it, he would have surely remembered what happened to the Philistines when they captured the Ark and "the hand of God was very heavy" upon them (see 1 Sm 5:11), or how Uzzah was instantaneously struck dead simply for touching the Ark (2 Sm 6:7). Who would have the temerity to bring the Ark into his home without clear instruction from God? A sound plan — a humble, pious plan — would seem to be to divorce Mary quietly instead. Doing so would avoid any shame for her (since people would assume the child was his) while avoiding incurring divine wrath for violating something holy in any way.

Saint Thomas Aquinas rightly connects Saint Joseph's reaction to that of Saint Peter, after Jesus' first miraculous catch of fish: "But when Simon Peter saw it, he fell down at Jesus' knees, saying, 'Depart from me, for I am a sinful man, O Lord.' For he was astonished, and all that were with him, at the catch of fish which they had taken; and so also were James and John, sons of Zebedee, who were partners with Simon. And Jesus said to Simon, 'Do not be afraid; henceforth you will be catching men' " (Lk 5:8–10).

Peter begged Jesus to leave, not because he thought Jesus was wicked, but because he thought Jesus was too holy. Likewise, after the Israelites saw God's glory and heard him speaking to Moses, they said, "We have this day seen God speak with man and man still live" and begged Moses to speak to God elsewhere, saying, "Why should we die? For this great fire will consume us; if we hear the voice of the LORD our God any more, we shall die" (Dt 5:24, 25). Even the prophet Isaiah, after seeing God, cried out, "Woe is me! For I am lost; for I am a man of unclean lips, and I dwell in the midst of a people of unclean lips; for my eyes have seen the King, the LORD of hosts!" (Is 6:5).

This is a healthy response to being in the presence of the holy numinous. Throughout Scripture, this is how the faithful reacted to Jacob's ladder, to the Ark of the Covenant, to the tabernacle, and to the Holy of Holies. Yet, as the early Christians realized, each of these things was only a foreshadowing of the Virgin Mary. (The Akathistos, an ancient hymn[10] used in the Byzantine liturgy, addresses Mary as the "celestial ladder by which God descended"[11] as well as the "tabernacle of God and the Word," "greater than the Holy of Holies," and the "ark gilded by the Spirit."[12]) That Joseph would want Mary to depart from him because he is a sinful man is precisely what we would expect if Joseph is also a just man.

But if all of this is true, why does the angel go on to say, "That which is conceived in her is of the Holy Spirit"? On its face, that might seem to match up better with the theory that Joseph suspected adultery. But there's another way of reading it. In all of the other instances when Jesus or an angel says, "Do not be afraid" or "Do not fear," they're not saying, "Do not be afraid, because there's nothing to fear." Jesus doesn't reply to Peter, for instance, by telling him that he's not really a sinner. Both of them know otherwise. Instead, he says, "Do not be afraid; henceforth you will be catching men" (Lk 5:10). Despite the fact that, humanly speaking, Peter has plenty of reason to fear, God is still merciful to him and is calling him into divine service. That would seem to be the message of the angel to Joseph as well: Yes, that which is conceived in Mary is of the Holy Spirit, but fear not, because God wants to use Joseph nevertheless, and he shall name the baby Jesus.

PRAYER

In this chapter, we looked at what Scripture does (and doesn't) mean in calling Saint Joseph "just" or "righteous." One of the passages that we didn't look at is Matthew 13:16–17, in which Jesus says, "Blessed are your eyes, for they see, and your ears, for they hear. Truly, I say to you, many prophets and righteous men longed to see what you see, and did not see it, and to hear what you hear, and did not hear it." When Jesus refers (positively) to "righteous men," that word "righteous" is *dikaios*, the same Greek word translated as "just."

This is the background behind a beautiful short prayer to Saint Joseph, one of the preparatory prayers for Mass. Pope Saint John Paul II shared this prayer with the world during his 1997 visit to the Shrine of St. Joseph in Kalisz, Poland.[13] In the Mass, the priest will hold the Body of Christ in his hands, and so he first says a prayer to the first man who ever had the chance to do that, Saint Joseph:

> O happy man, Saint Joseph, whose privilege it was
> not only to see and hear that God whom many a

king has longed to see, yet saw not, longed to hear, yet heard not (cf. Mt 13:17); but also to carry him in your arms and kiss him, to clothe him and watch over him!

QUESTIONS

1. Where in my life have I experienced something numinous in the way that C. S. Lewis describes: an experience of holiness that made me realize my unworthiness?

2. What would it have been like for Saint Joseph, as a faithful Jew, to live in the same house as the Virgin Mary and Jesus? How would I have responded to that situation?

3. Does my approach to the Eucharist and to the Mass reflect that, like Saint Joseph, I am "not worthy to have you [Jesus] come under my roof" (Mt 8:8)?

4. Am I more likely to forget my sinfulness, or to forget that God is bigger than my sinfulness and wants to use me nevertheless?

5. What are some of the ways in which God seems to want to use me, if I will simply let him?

5.

Joseph, the Father
of Jesus?

If the problem before the Annunciation was figuring out whether Saint Joseph was the true spouse of Mary, the problem afterward is figuring out whether he was the true father of Jesus. At first, it may not seem so. After all, both Saint Matthew and Saint Luke tell us that Jesus was born of a virgin, and Luke begins his account of the public years of Christ by saying that "Jesus, when he began his ministry, was about thirty years of age, being the son (as was supposed) of Joseph" (Lk 3:23). And yet it's clear that the Church treats Saint Joseph not only as a true father but as the patron saint of fathers.[1] In some Catholic countries, Saint Joseph's feast day, March 19, is Father's Day.[2] So which is it? Was Saint

Joseph a model father or not a father at all? As you might suspect, a lot turns on what you mean by the question.

SAINT JOSEPH, THE FATHER OF JESUS

Under Jewish law, there were certain cases in which it was perfectly acceptable to have one father biologically and another one legally. For instance, in the case of levirate marriage, if a man died childless, his brother was encouraged to marry his widow "and perform the duty of a husband's brother to her. And the first son whom she bears shall succeed to the name of his brother who is dead, that his name may not be blotted out of Israel" (Dt 25:5–6). Here, the living brother was the biological father, but the dead brother was the legally recognized father, and in this way his name and house were carried on.

We should have this in the back of our minds when we look at the messianic prophecies. On the one hand, there's the prophecy through Isaiah that the Messiah would be born of a virgin (see Is 7:10–14). That's a prophecy about the Messiah's *biological* fatherhood. But on the other hand, there is a whole series of prophecies about the Messiah's being of the line of David, which is a question of *legal* fatherhood. For instance, God had promised King David that "when your days are fulfilled and you lie down with your fathers, I will raise up your offspring after you, who shall come forth from your body, and I will establish his kingdom." Moreover, unlike the house of Saul (David's predecessor, whose royal line ended), "your house and your kingdom shall be made sure for ever before me; your throne shall be established for ever" (2 Sm 7:12, 16). When the angel Gabriel declares that the child to be born "will be great, and will be called the Son of the Most High; / and the Lord God will give to him the throne of his father David" (Lk 1:32), this is the proph-

ecy being referenced. But this prophecy is fulfilled because
Mary is married "to a man whose name was Joseph, of the
house of David" (Lk 1:27).

Pope John Paul II explained that "while it is important
for the Church to profess the virginal conception of Jesus,
it is no less important to uphold Mary's marriage to Joseph,
because juridically Joseph's fatherhood depends on it."[3] If
you err in one direction (thinking of Saint Joseph as Jesus'
biological father), then you end up denying Isaiah 7. But if
you err in the opposite direction (thinking of Joseph as only
the presumed father of Jesus), then you end up denying 2
Samuel 7 and the other Davidic prophecies. This would also
be an unchristian view of family and fatherhood, as Saint
Augustine explains: "We can't say that Joseph wasn't a father,
just because he never slept with the mother of the Lord —
as though it were lust that made someone into a wife, and
not married love."[4] And so a healthy Christian response is to
embrace Joseph as a true father to Jesus, even as we recognize that this fatherhood wasn't biological.

This is also the biblical witness. Almost immediately after detailing the virginal conception and birth of Jesus, Saint
Luke goes on to tell how "*the parents* brought in the child
Jesus, to do for him according to the custom of the law" by
bringing him to the Temple. Luke also refers to Joseph and
Mary as "his father and his mother" (Lk 2:33). When they
find Jesus in the Temple, years later, Mary says to him, "Behold, your father and I have been looking for you anxiously"
(Lk 2:48). As Saint Augustine points out, the Virgin Mary
was "perfectly well aware that she had not conceived Christ
by Joseph's conjugal embrace" (no one could be in less doubt
about the Virgin Birth than she!), but even she calls Joseph
Christ's father.[5]

It's Jesus' response to Mary's words that have confused

many Christians. In the Greek text, Jesus literally says, "Did you not know that I must be about my Father's?" This line has been translated into English as "about my Father's business" or "in my Father's house," both of which make sense grammatically and contextually.[6] Either way, it might look at first as if Jesus is rebuking Mary and disowning Joseph as a father, by saying that his *true* father is God the Father. But Augustine points out that this interpretation misses the broader context: Jesus then "went down with them and came to Nazareth, and was obedient to them" (Lk 2:51). Jesus simultaneously honors the fatherhood of Joseph and the fatherhood of God the Father, and his obedient submission to both is perfect. Rather than rejecting Joseph's fatherhood, Jesus affirms it, but in a way that helps us to make sense of it.

Indeed, one of the most radical aspects of the Gospel is the insistence that *spiritual* fatherhood is more important than *biological* fatherhood. When some of Jesus' Jewish opponents insist that "Abraham is our father," Jesus responds by rejecting this claim: "If you were Abraham's children, you would do what Abraham did" (Jn 8:39). And when a woman in the crowd shouts to Jesus, "Blessed is the womb that bore you, and the breasts that you sucked!," he replies, "Blessed rather are those who hear the word of God and keep it!" (Lk 11:27, 28). His point is not (as some Protestants have argued) to denigrate Mary or to argue that she isn't blessed. She plainly is (see Lk 1:42). His point is *why* she's blessed: not because of her blood ties to Jesus, but because of her faith. As Elizabeth said at the Visitation, "Blessed is she who believed that there would be a fulfillment of what was spoken to her from the Lord" (Lk 1:45). At every turn, Jesus shows that the most important family is the adoptive, spiritual family.

This is tremendous news for all of us, whether we are

adoptive fathers or not. Why? Because all of us are adoptive children. As Saint Paul reminds us, the Father sent Christ "to redeem those who were under the law, so that we might receive adoption as sons" (Gal 4:5). To suggest that Saint Joseph isn't a "true" father to Jesus because he's an adoptive father is an argument that's fundamentally incompatible with Christianity. Every time we pray the Lord's Prayer, we dare to call upon our own adoptive Father in the words "Our Father."

THE FATHERHOOD OF SAINT JOSEPH

Saying that Joseph is the *legal* father of Jesus may sound like legalism, or as if the evangelists found some sort of technicality to make the messianic prophecies fit together. That would be a mistake. Rather, this meant that "the Word of God was humbly subject to Joseph, that he obeyed him, and that he rendered to him all those offices that children are bound to render to their parents," and that "Joseph became the guardian, the administrator, and the legal defender of the divine house whose chief he was."[7] This is at once a profound theological reality and an immensely practical one. As we've just seen, Jesus — the Creator of all things — voluntarily submitted to Saint Joseph as his father. Saint Bernard of Clairvaux describes the paradox well: "the Master obeying his disciples, God obeying men, God's Word and Wisdom obeying a carpenter and his wife."[8] The fact that Jesus was known in the community both as "the carpenter's son" (Mt 13:55) and "the carpenter" (Mk 6:3) points us to the depths of Christ's humility and his intimacy with Saint Joseph: that he would be so associated with him that he would be known as Joseph's son, and that he, Divine Wisdom incarnate, would allow himself to be taught carpentry by Joseph and then make his living in imitation of his earthly father. And Christ's humility required a tremendous humility on the part of Saint Joseph as well, to be able to command and instruct the Son he knew to be God.

Of course, this meant that Saint Joseph's fatherhood was utterly unique in some obvious ways. After all, it was to "assure fatherly protection for Jesus that God chose Joseph to be Mary's spouse,"[9] a task that meant everything up to and including guarding "from death the Child threatened by a monarch's jealousy," a struggle that most of us thankfully never have to face.[10] But in other ways, the call of Joseph's fatherhood looks very familiar to any Christian father. For instance, as the father of the family, it would have been Joseph's responsibility to lead the family in morning, meal, and evening prayers, and Jesus would have gone with Joseph to the synagogue.[11] Pope Paul VI described Joseph as expressing his fatherhood "in having used the legal authority which was his over the Holy Family in order to make a total gift of self, of his life and work; in having turned his human vocation to domestic love into a superhuman oblation of self, an oblation of his heart and all his abilities into love placed at the service of the Messiah growing up in his house."[12]

Throughout it all, Joseph remained "ever the companion, the assistance, and the upholder of the Virgin and of Jesus."[13] In one sense, this is a singular calling, unlike any given before or since in the history of the world. But in another sense, it's the calling given to every father: Take care of your family, and remain close to Jesus and Mary in the process. The only real difference is that, for Joseph, this was one commandment rather than two.

This explains why Pope Benedict XVI and others have argued that Joseph is a model for priests and other spiritual fathers. He's "a father, without fatherhood according to the flesh" who nevertheless "lives his fatherhood fully and completely," and his only reward "was to be with Christ."[14] So what can biological and spiritual fathers learn from Saint Joseph? For starters, how to recognize their place as "shadows of the Father."

SHADOWS OF THE FATHER

What makes Saint Joseph distinct — and, as we'll see, what makes him utterly indistinct — from other fathers is that he's not the father of Jesus in the fullest sense of the term. Without denying Joseph's fatherhood, Jesus can nevertheless reply to his mother's words by pointing to the one who is his Father in a fuller sense: God the Father (see Lk 2:48–49). Pope Francis, drawing upon the Polish writer Jan Dobraczyński, refers to Saint Joseph as "the earthly shadow of the heavenly Father," an image that powerfully captures Joseph's fatherly role.[15]

On the surface, it might seem as if Saint Joseph's being a sort of stand-in for God the Father would make him a poor model for fathers. But on the contrary, it's precisely because of this that he reveals something important about the dimensions of human fatherhood. Cardinal Timothy Dolan tells a story of stopping for the night with the Dominicans in Zanesville, Ohio, and commenting to one of the "crusty but wise" old friars, "Your room is so plain, where do you keep the rest of your stuff?" The friar pointed out that Dolan had only a suitcase. Dolan replied, "Well, sure, but, after all, I'm just passing through," to which the friar said, "Aren't we all?"[16] Likewise, when we're tempted to say of Saint Joseph, "But he's is only standing in the place of the true father, God the Father!" the appropriate reply is, "Aren't we all?"

In the *Summa Theologiae*, Saint Thomas Aquinas points out that there are two types of names for God.[17] In the first type, we use earthly things to describe God — for instance, we call Christ "the Lion of the tribe of Judah" (Rv 5:5) or the "Rock" (1 Cor 10:4). In these cases, lion and rock literally refer to earthly realities, and only by analogy or metaphor refer to divine realities. There's some sense in which Christ is like a lion or like a rock. But in the other cases, when we call God good, we don't mean that analogously. Good literally applies only to God, for "no one is good but God alone" (Mk 10:18). In this case, the analogy runs in the other direction. When Scripture says that Barnabas is "a good man" (Acts 11:24), for instance, it doesn't mean that he's infinite, perfect goodness in the way that God is. It means simply that he shares in and reflects God's goodness in some particular way.

In which category is the word *father*? We might think that when we call God *Father*, we mean that he's sort of like earthly fathers. But Scripture says the opposite: *Only* God is Father, and when we call anyone on earth *father*, we mean it only analogously, the way we do when we call them *good*. As Pope Francis points out, this is the meaning of Jesus' admonition to "call no man your father on earth, for you have one Father, who is in heaven" (Mt 23:9). When other people in Scripture are called father — for example, in Romans 4:16 and 1 Corinthians 4:15 — it means only that they are in some way a sharer in the one fatherhood of God, revealing to us through their lives what it means for God to be our Father. And this is also what Saint Paul means when he says, "For this reason I bow my knees before the Father [*Patēr*], from whom every family [*patria*] in heaven and on earth is named" (Eph 3:14–15).

Fathers are at their best when they realize that they don't deserve the title father and embrace their fatherhood as "a 'sign' pointing to a greater fatherhood," and a chance to be "a shadow of the heavenly Father."[18] This is true of biological and spiritual fathers alike. The Letter to the Hebrews admonishes us to "obey your leaders and submit to them; for they are keeping watch over your souls, as men who will have to give account" (Heb 13:17). It is when earthly fathers forget this by thinking of the family or parish as their private possession, for their personal enjoyment or abuse, that problems arise. Steven Tracy recalled a moment from his time as an evangelical pastor when he asked a member of his congregation why he continued to sexually abuse his children, even while out on parole. To Tracy's horror, the man replied, "I guess I did it because I was the head of the family, and it was my right to do whatever I wanted to my wife and kids."[19] But that is precisely *not* what Christianity teaches. Rather, biological and spiritual fathers alike are stand-ins for the one, true Father, to whom they shall one day give account for how they treated *his* children.

Indeed, the Holy Family is exactly to whom we should look to better understand controversial questions such as what it means to believe in a father's "headship" over his family (see Eph 5:21–33). It's easy to fall into the trap of thinking either that (a) since the Bible presents the man as the head of the family, Christians must think that "father knows best" and that he's the wisest and holiest member of the family; or (b) when the father plainly isn't the wisest or holiest, he therefore shouldn't be acknowledged as head. But Saint Joseph was entrusted with "fatherly authority over Jesus,"[20] even though he had no pretense of being the holiest or wisest member of the Holy Family. Joseph shows us that true headship is grounded precisely in a healthy sense of one's own unworthiness. It's a healthy reminder that those in authority should be the first to admit that "we are unworthy servants; we have only done what was our duty" (Lk 17:10).

Properly understood, such a message is liberating for

fathers. When we forget who is truly in charge, we start trying to take control ourselves, creating an overly restrictive
atmosphere in our homes and parishes. Lenore Skenazy and
Jonathan Haidt have argued persuasively that "by trying to
keep children safe from all risks, obstacles, hurt feelings,
and fears, our culture has taken away the opportunities they
need to become successful adults. In treating them as fragile
— emotionally, socially, and physically — society actually
makes them so." We need to recall the old proverb "prepare
your child for the path, not the path for your child."[21] Saint
Joseph reminds us that we are but shadows of the father and
that a father's job is ultimately to become "useless."[22] One
of the finest examples of this comes from Pope John XXIII,
who, at the end of the day, would go before the Blessed Sacrament and pray, "Lord, I've done the best I could today. It's
your Church. I'm going to bed."[23] Would that parents would
take the same attitude in their families, entrusting the care
of their children to their true Father!

PRAYER
At the end of chapter three, we prayed the first of three
prayers that Saint John Henry Newman composed on the
"Glorious Titles of St. Joseph." Here are his prayers[24] for the
second title, "Father of the Son of God":

> His was the title of father of the Son of God, because
> he was the Spouse of Mary, ever Virgin. He was Our
> Lord's father, because Jesus ever yielded to him
> the obedience of a son. He was Our Lord's father,
> because to him were entrusted, and by him were
> faithfully fulfilled, the duties of a father, in protect-
> ing him, giving him a home, sustaining and rearing
> him, and providing him with a trade.

V. Blessed be the name of Joseph.
R. Henceforth and forever. Amen.

Let us pray.
God, who in thine ineffable Providence didst vouchsafe to choose Blessed Joseph to be the husband of thy most holy Mother, grant, we beseech thee, that we may be made worthy to receive him for our intercessor in heaven, whom on earth we venerate as our holy Protector: who livest and reignest world without end. Amen.

QUESTIONS

1. Who are the fathers whom God has placed in my life, and how have they served as earthly shadows of my heavenly Father? What have their witnesses revealed to me about God?

2. In those places where God has entrusted me with authority (in my family, church, community, etc.), how can I keep in view the fact that I am serving simply as one who must give account?

3. Who is someone who lives out earthly headship well? What is it about his example that is compelling?

4. Do I trust that God is in control even of those areas in which I have responsibilities, or do I feel a need to control everything?

6.

Creative Courage and the Silence of God

A nother concrete manifestation of Saint Joseph's father-hood can be seen in the flight into Egypt. The scriptural account is remarkably short, essentially three verses. An angel appeared to Joseph in a dream and gave him the following message: "Rise, take the child and his mother, and flee to Egypt, and remain there till I tell you; for Herod is about to search for the child, to destroy him" (Mt 2:13). Asking no questions, Joseph "rose and took the child and his mother by night, and departed to Egypt, and remained there until the death of Herod" (Mt 2:14–15).

In the often-tense political environment surrounding immigration, it can be controversial to call the Holy Family refugees,[1] but that is what they were. In "the drama of having to flee to Egypt because of the homicidal fury of Herod,"[2] the family escaped Herod's jurisdiction by fleeing to a neighboring land. Indeed, Pope Pius XII declared:

> The émigré Holy Family of Nazareth, fleeing into Egypt, is the archetype of every refugee family. Jesus, Mary, and Joseph, living in exile in Egypt to escape the fury of an evil king, are, for all times and all places, the models and protectors of every migrant, alien and refugee of whatever kind who, whether compelled by fear of persecution or by want, is forced to leave his native land, his beloved parents and relatives, his close friends, and to seek a foreign soil.[3]

This is important for us to remember, not only because it helps to humanize refugees and migrants (which is important), but also because it helps to drive home what an awful experience the flight into Egypt likely was. The Holy Family was leaving family, Joseph's job, all of the people they knew, their local synagogue, the society that spoke their native language, and more. We know that they ordinarily "went to Jerusalem every year at the feast of the Passover" (Lk 2:41), but even that would be on hold. Those of us who missed out on Easter Mass in 2020 due to COVID-19 may have a glimmer of that particular deprivation, except that we still had the solace of streamed Masses.

But it's not just that the flight into Egypt was difficult; it's that it involved countless decisions for which the angel simply hadn't prepared Saint Joseph. The author of an Advent reflection, musing on all the decisions she struggles to make, envied Saint Joseph and asked, "Wouldn't it be nice if

an angel told us what to do in a dream?"[4] But the remarkable thing about Saint Joseph's dream is the *lack* of detailed
instructions. For starters, there were two main routes to
Egypt. The more traveled one "passed through Gaza and
then ran south along the Mediterranean coast," while the
other "passed through Hebron and Bersabee before crossing
the Idumean desert and entering the Sinai peninsula."[5] Was
it safe for the family to take the easier road and hope they
would avoid Herod's soldiers? Or should they take the road
through the desert and hope they would avoid bandits and
desert heat? Or should they, as some traditions claim, find
an even more obscure route?[6]

And once they escaped Judea, where should they go in
Egypt? Was this to be a short stay, during which they should
lie low? Or should they settle in for the long haul? Should
Saint Joseph attempt to get into business as a carpenter?
Should they stay in inns or try to buy a house? Pope Francis
has pointed out that "the Gospel does not tell us how long
Mary, Joseph, and the child remained in Egypt," but that
"they certainly needed to eat, to find a home and employ-
ment."[7] And amid all of these major life changes, the angel of
the Lord fell silent, leaving only the instructions to "remain
there till I tell you."

Even if you've never lived as a refugee, there's a good
chance that you have faced life decisions about where to live
and work, or your vocation, or any number of big and small
questions about how best to follow God. And perhaps you've
experienced the frustration that C. S. Lewis described: that
God feels present when you "have no sense of needing him,"
but that you go to him "when your need is desperate, when
all other help is vain, and what do you find? A door slammed
in your face, and a sound of bolting and double bolting on
the inside. After that, silence."[8] Needless to say, this experi-

ence can be confusing and discouraging. So what are some of the pitfalls that we fall into when facing such decisions, and what's the better way that Saint Joseph models for us?

HOW TO DECIDE WELL (OR NOT)

Most of us have never stopped to think about just what goes into decision-making. But Saint Thomas Aquinas described any prudent action as having three stages: deliberation, judgment, and action.[9] You gather the facts, figure out the right thing to do, and then do it. Of course, that will look different in different contexts: Deciding your thesis topic might take more (and different) work than figuring out where to meet a friend for coffee. But it's good to have these three basic steps in mind to help us think about our thinking more clearly. We can ask, "Should I still be gathering facts or seeking counsel?" "Am I ready to decide?" "Should I be carrying out the decision that I made?" It's possible to go off the rails in either direction during each of these three stages.

We can deliberate too little by rushing to make a decision before we have all the facts. But we can also deliberate too much, allowing our spiritual growth to be choked by "the cares of the world" (Mt 13:22). Not for nothing does Jesus instruct us: "Do not be anxious, saying, 'What shall we eat?' or 'What shall we drink?' or 'What shall we wear?'" (Mt 6:31). And when we do decide upon a plan of action, are we too flexible or inflexible in carrying it out? That is, are we more likely to fall into the trap of failing to follow through on good resolutions, or on sticking to our guns even when circumstances change and prudence would dictate a change of plans?

It's important for each of us to know how we personally tend to err in the decision-making process, and in which direction, so that we can correct for it. Aristotle says that "we must drag ourselves away to the contrary extreme."[10] To use an analogy, you need to determine whether your car's alignment drifts to the left or to the right, so you know in which direction you need to actively correct in order to keep on a straight path.

Our natural decision-making tendencies make an important difference in the spiritual life, particularly in the realm of prayer and discernment. Many of us have the problem of acting first and praying later, or of asking God for forgiveness rather than permission, or simply of sectioning off whole areas of our lives that we think of as under "our" control and don't even take to God. Yet this notion of prayer is backward. If prayer is conversation with God, then the first recorded prayer happens immediately after the Fall. Adam and Eve "heard the sound of the LORD God walking in the garden in the cool of the day" and hid themselves, and "the LORD God called to the man, and said to him, 'Where are you?' " (Gn 3:8, 9). That's the start of the first prayer. And the first difficulty in prayer is not that God is silent; the first difficulty is that sinful man doesn't want to hear what God has to say. God is the one calling out to man, not the other way around. Over the years, we've gotten better, and a good deal subtler, in our hiding from God. For me, and I suspect for many reading this book, it's not hiding from God in the bushes, but hiding from him in the calendar. It's saying that I'm "too busy" for prayer, even though I make time for countless other, less important things.

But there's a vice at the opposite extreme as well. Of course, it's not possible to pray too much, but it is possible to use prayer as an excuse not to act, particularly if I'm not feeling brave, or if my natural inclination is to overdeliberate — to spend too long in my head, and never have that materialize into firm action. In these cases, prayer can even be a pious cover for a lack of prudence. This is particularly acute in the realm of vocational discernment. Various priests and religious have identified a state of "perpetual discernment" as a serious problem for vocations to the priesthood and religious life, and I suspect that many single Catholics have found a similar problem among the opposite sex, or even among themselves, in pursuing marriage. The problem here is not that we're listening to God too much: it's that we're sitting on our hands and refusing to move forward until he answers us.

Some of us need to be reminded of Moses' words to the people of Israel at the edge of the Red Sea: "The LORD will fight for you, and you have only to be still" (Ex 14:14), while others need to be reminded of God's words in the very next verse: "Why do you cry to me? Tell the sons of Israel to go forward" (Ex 14:15).

One reason that this is so confusing is that sometimes God seems silent because we're not listening, but sometimes he seems silent because he's not giving us the answer that we're asking for. So what do we do if, after having done everything that we can to discern well, we still don't have a clear sense of what God is asking of us in all its particulars? Here's where the example of Saint Joseph is instructive, with the idea of what Pope Francis calls "creative courage."

CREATIVE COURAGE

It's remarkable, even shocking, that the Father seems to be silent even when the life of his own Son is threatened by Herod. But Pope Francis points out that God wasn't really silent; instead, Saint Joseph "was the true 'miracle,' by which God saves the child and his mother," and that "God acted by trusting in Joseph's creative courage."[11] This is a lesson to us, that "if at times God seems not to help us, surely this does not mean that we have been abandoned, but instead are being trusted to plan, to be creative, and to find solutions ourselves."[12] The pope illustrates this idea with the friends of the paralytic in Luke 5:17–26, who, faced with a crowd obstructing their ability to get to Jesus, simply climbed up on the roof and lowered their friend through it. They didn't let the obstacles stop them from getting to Jesus, nor did they simply sit and wait for a sign from God about how to act. Rather, they did what seemed right — not because they trusted in themselves, but because they trusted in Jesus.

That's creative courage in action, and there are countless other examples of this in Scripture. The God of Israel encourages a sort of feistiness, as we see in Jesus' back-and-forth with the Syrophoenician woman (see Mk 7:27–29) and in God's haggling with Abraham (Gn 18:16–33). The strange story of God's wrestling with Jacob (Gn 32:22–32) shows us both that it's okay to wrestle with God, and that God sometimes doesn't seem to fight fair (see v. 25). We're called to "pray and not lose heart," like the persistent widow who pestered the judge until he gave her what she wanted (Lk 18:1–8). But we're also called to act like the first two servants in the parable of the talents, in which God compares himself to a "man going on a journey" who entrusts his property to his servants (Mt 25:14). He leaves no clear instructions, but leaves them money (coins called *talents*, the origin of the English word), "to each according to his ability. Then he went away" (Mt 25:15). The first two servants act with creative courage, using the talents that were entrusted to them profitably, and are praised by their master as "good and faithful" servants upon his return. But often, we want to act like the "wicked and slothful servant," by burying our talents, lest we make a mistake in investing them (Mt 25:21, 23, 26). Often we need to be reminded that "God did not give us a spirit of timidity but a spirit of power and love and self-control" (2 Tm 1:7).

This is why it's important that God has left us with the witness of both the Virgin Mary and Saint Joseph.[13] With Mary, we get a clear reminder of the priority of prayer, and that all of our actions should be rooted in (and flow from) a life of interior intimacy with God. Mary is open to God and receives what he has for her with docility, and it's precisely this that enables her to arise and go with haste to tend to the needs of her relative Elizabeth (see Lk 1:38–40). But there are times in which it's neither appropriate nor feasible to stop to pray. The flight into Egypt is an obvious example: If Joseph had stopped to wait for a sign at every turn in the road, the family would never have escaped. And so Joseph shows us what it looks like to be open to God amid action, particularly in such times and places, and of the role of creative courage in putting God's plan into action. Perhaps the New Testament figure most akin to Joseph in this regard is Saint Paul, who seems to be always on the move, but is ready at a moment's notice to change directions if it seems God is calling him elsewhere (see, for example, Acts 18:23; 1 Cor 16:7; 2 Cor 1:15—2:4). Both men show us what it looks like to avoid the two poles of idly waiting for divine revelation, on the one hand, and trying to be the lords of our own lives, on the other.

Perhaps it's not a coincidence that we see Saint Joseph living this creative courage in the context of his fatherhood. God has given him the general command to take care of Jesus and Mary, but then Joseph has to figure out all the details along the way. What parent cannot relate to this? As we saw in the last chapter, one of the tasks of parents (and particularly of fathers) is to reveal to their children what a loving father looks like, so that these children will more readily believe in a loving Father. The burden of this can feel daunting at times, and each day is filled with new challenges: "How should I respond to this behavior?"; "Should I grant this request?"; and so on. It's impossible to pause each moment and run to the chapel, so what's needed is the development of a spirit capable of discernment in motion, as well as a faith that believes God can work through us when we're doing everything we can to be docile to his will, even when we don't really know what we're doing.

Of course, it's important to remember that Joseph isn't just a man of action. He is also a man of prayer and of quiet receptivity. Even as he is acting, he is waiting: waiting on the Lord and waiting on the angel to return. How do we know this? Because the moment the angel does return, he leaves all of his activity behind and pursues a new set of plans based on what he has received. After Herod died, an angel appeared to Joseph in a dream, saying, "Rise, take the child and his mother, and go to the land of Israel, for those who sought the child's life are dead" (Mt 2:20). As before, Joseph "rose and took the child and his mother, and went to the land of Israel" (Mt 2:21). This tremendous docility to God is the hallmark of true interior freedom. It is also evidence of Joseph's deep interior life, which equipped him to lead the life to which God called him.

We need to learn from this as well. The idea of discernment in motion is not a rejection of the fact that we need to create the time and space to "go into your room and shut the door and pray to your Father who is in secret" (Mt 6:6). Saint Paul tells us to "pray constantly" (1 Thes 5:17), but as the *Catechism* points out, "we cannot pray 'at all times' if we do not pray at specific times, consciously willing it" (2697). In a busy world, we need to learn to pray amid busyness. But we also need to learn to leave the busyness aside at times and to be with God. Joseph was repeatedly called to action, but he received these calls in the silence of night. We must not be afraid to act, to use our talents as best we can, but we must also not forget to make space for the silence in which we can hear the "still small voice" of God (see 1 Kgs 19:12).

PRAYER

In chapter four, I mentioned an ancient Byzantine prayer, called an *Akathistos* hymn, to the Virgin Mary. There's also an *Akathistos* (or *Akathist*) hymn to Saint Joseph,[14] and I want to highlight a small part of it for us to pray, both because I think it captures the creative courage that Saint Joseph models, and because I think it will serve as a good segue for our final chapter, in which we unpack the connections between our Joseph and the Old Testament patriarch of the same name:

> Desiring to save from the malice of Herod, him that had come to save the world, O wondrous Joseph, you did not question the angel that commanded you to flee into Egypt, by saying: "Could he that saves others not save himself"? But being a man of faith, like a new Abraham, ever ready for obedience, giving no thought to the rigors of the journey, nor considering the time of return, you did straightway take yourself to Egypt with Mary and the Babe, joyously crying out to God: ALLELUIA!
>
> In Egypt you were shown to be a new Joseph, greater than the patriarch of old, who saved the people of Egypt from famine; for you saved from death the Savior of the world and offered unto the people of Egypt, who were starving amidst the famine of godlessness, the Bread of Life; and

you sowed the seed of eternal life, whence a wondrous harvest sprang forth in the deserts of Egypt. Therefore we cry to you:

Rejoice! You joyfully endured sorrows and labors on the way, for Christ's sake!
Rejoice! O guardian of the infant Jesus who once guided Israel in the wilderness with the pillar of fire and a cloud!
Rejoice! Nourisher of him that sustained his people with manna!
Rejoice! You who bore in your arms the Creator and Sustainer of all creation!
Rejoice! You who did save from the malice of Herod him that once saved the people of God from the bitter bondage to Pharaoh!
Rejoice! You who showed forth for Egypt the grace of adoption instead of slavery!
Rejoice! O righteous Joseph, ready helper and intercessor for our souls!

QUESTIONS

1. Saint Thomas Aquinas describes the three parts of making a prudent decision as deliberation (gathering the facts), judgment (figuring out what to do), and action (doing it). When I deliberate, do I tend to give things too much thought or too little thought?

2. Do I tend toward the extreme of trying to do everything by myself (and forgetting to pray) or of refusing to act until God makes everything crystal clear?

3. When I pray and God still seems silent, how do I respond?

4. Which people in my life live out "creative courage"? What is it about their witness that speaks to me?

7.

Ite ad Ioseph

In 2017, I had the opportunity to visit the beautiful Chiesa di San Giuseppe dei Padri Teatini (Church of Saint Joseph of the Theatine Fathers) in Palermo, Sicily, on the feast of Saint Joseph. The Sicilians have had a tremendous devotion to Saint Joseph for centuries, after his intercession ended one of the island's terrible droughts. As one author has noted, "Wherever Sicilian immigrants settled [in America], Saint Joseph came with them."[1] This church in Palermo is ornately adorned, celebrating the life and faith of Saint Joseph, but one door in particular jumped out to me, because it was engraved with the words *Ite ad Ioseph*, a Latin expression meaning "go to Joseph." As Pope Francis has pointed out, this phrase has become associated with "popular trust in Saint Joseph."[2]

"Go to Joseph" is a line from the Bible, but it wasn't originally about Saint Joseph. It comes from the book of Gene-
sis, in which Pharaoh said to the Egyptians, "Go to Joseph;
what he says to you, do" (Gn 41:55). The Joseph in question
was the patriarch Joseph, the son of Jacob. On the surface, it
might look as if the Bible is being quoted out of context: a
verse about one Joseph being applied to another. In reality,
it's a good example of how to read Scripture properly.

We see something similar at play in the account of the
flight into Egypt, when Saint Matthew says that it "was to
fulfil what the Lord had spoken by the prophet, 'Out of Egypt
have I called my son' " (Mt 2:15). Matthew is quoting Hosea
11, in which the "son" is very explicitly Israel: "When Israel
was a child, I loved him, / and out of Egypt I called my son.
/ The more I called them, / the more they went from me; /
they kept sacrificing to the Baals, / and burning incense to
idols" (vv. 1–2). Again, it looks as if Bible verses are being
taken out of their proper context. But in reality both the New
Testament authors and the early Church Fathers show us that
"the New Testament lies hidden in the Old and the Old Testament is unveiled in the New" (CCC 129). In some ways, the
various Old Testament stories prefigure events in the New
Testament and in the moral life. This is how Saint Paul can,
for instance, read the story of the Exodus as a story about the
sacraments and faith and conclude that these things "were
written down for our instruction" (see 1 Cor 10:1–13).

Understood in this way, why have so many Christians
seen a connection between the two Josephs, and what can
the Joseph of the Old Testament reveal for us about the Joseph of the New?

THE TWO JOSEPHS
At a surface level, of course, the Old Testament patriarch

Joseph and the New Testament Saint Joseph share a name, and both of them have fathers named Jacob (see Mt 1:16; Gn 46:19). But the parallels run deeper. The patriarch Joseph's brothers mocked him as a "dreamer" (Gn 37:19), and the course of his life was dictated, in no small part, by both his own prophetic dreams (Gn 37:5–11) and the dreams that he interpreted (Gn 40–41). Likewise, God spoke to Saint Joseph through prophetic dreams (Mt 1:19–25; 2:13–15, 19–23).

Both Josephs were also betrayed by those they should have been able to trust, resulting in escapes into Egypt. The Old Testament patriarch's own brothers plotted against him, saying, "Let us kill him and throw him into one of the pits; then we shall say that a wild beast has devoured him, and we shall see what will become of his dreams" (Gn 37:20). This plot was averted by one of the brothers, Reuben, and the brothers decided to sell Joseph into slavery instead. In this way, he ended up being sold to "Potiphar, an officer of Pharaoh, the captain of the guard" (Gn 37:36) in the land of Egypt. The New Testament Joseph was betrayed by his own king, but, being warned through a dream, he and his family escaped, ending up as refugees in Egypt (see Mt 2:13–14). In this way, it was prophetic dreams that led both Josephs into Egypt, and it would be prophetic dreams that brought them back again. For the patriarch, it was his ability to interpret Pharaoh's dreams that led to his rising from slave to vizier of Egypt and gave him the freedom to go up to the Promised Land to bury his father (Gn 50:4–14). For Saint Joseph, it was a pair of dreams in which angels led him back to the Promised Land and ultimately into the town of Nazareth (Mt 2:19–23).

There's also something incomplete or unfinished about the lives of both Josephs; or, if you prefer, both Josephs saw forward, past their own deaths, to divine visitation. On his deathbed, the patriarch Joseph prophesied to his family, "God will visit you, and you shall carry up my bones from here" (Gn 50:25). The Letter to the Hebrews points to this as evidence of Joseph's faith and a prophecy of "the exodus of the Israelites" (Heb 11:22). Sure enough, while Joseph was originally buried in Egypt (see Gn 50:26), the descendants of Joseph never forgot their promise, and four hundred years later, Moses brought the bones of Joseph out of Egypt during the Exodus (Ex 13:19; Jos 24:32). Likewise, at the presentation in the Temple, the prophet Simeon (looking forward to his own death), had declared, "Lord, now let your servant depart in peace, according to your word; for my eyes have seen your salvation which you have prepared in the presence of all peoples, a light for revelation to the Gentiles, and for glory to your people Israel"; and we're told that Jesus' "father and his mother marveled at what was said about him" (Lk 2:29–33). This prophecy would come true, but Joseph wouldn't live long enough to see it. The last we hear of Joseph is in the finding in the Temple, when Jesus was twelve. Sometime between then and the beginning of Jesus' public ministry, eighteen years later, Joseph died.

THE LOWEST PLACE AT THE TABLE

So what can we learn from the two Josephs? Often in life we want to run from our sufferings and our trials, but as Pope Francis has pointed out, "the flight into Egypt caused by Herod's threat shows us that God is present where man is in danger, where man is suffering, where he is fleeing, where he experiences rejection and abandonment."[3] Upon their entry into Egypt, neither Joseph is under any illusion of being the master of his own destiny. One enters the country as a slave; the other as a refugee awaiting further divine revelation. It's safe to say that neither man would have seen his life ending up there. Before this moment, each Joseph had received a divine revelation that seemed to bode well. The first Joseph had a dream in which "the sun, the moon, and eleven stars were bowing down to me" (Gn 37:9) representing his elevation over the rest of his family. The second Joseph was promised by an angel that his wife would "bear a son, and you shall call his name Jesus, for he will save his people from their sins" (Mt 1:21). But now the first Joseph's family has sold him into slavery, and the second Joseph is keeping his son and Savior from the hands of a bloodthirsty tyrant.

Saint John Chrysostom points out that it would have been easy for Saint Joseph to object to the angel: Christ is supposed to save his people from their sins, and he can't even save himself?[4] Indeed, there are several moments in the lives of both Josephs when it would have been easy for them to fall into bitterness and resentment — at God, the world, or the people who betrayed them. But instead, they stayed humble and close to God. The Book of Wisdom says that when the patriarch Joseph was sold into slavery, holy Wisdom "did not desert him, / but delivered him from sin. / She descended with him into the dungeon, / and when he was in prison she did not leave him, / until she brought him the scepter of a kingdom / and authority over his masters" (Wis 10:13–14). Likewise, Chrysostom described how, on their flight into Egypt, Joseph and Mary had "a great fellow-traveler, the Child that had been born."[5] That child, of course, is Jesus Christ, "Divine Wisdom incarnate."[6]

By trusting in God's Wisdom, both Josephs persevered even in the face of bleak circumstances. Time would show that God permitted them to go through these trials for a reason. These times of hardship were for their good, for the good of their families, and for the good of the whole world, in ways they could never have foreseen. In the words of the psalmist, when the Lord "summoned a famine on the land, / and broke every staff of bread, / he had sent a man ahead of them, / Joseph, who was sold as a slave" (Ps 105:16–17).[7] But the Josephs couldn't see this in the midst of their own trials; they had to take God at his word.

After the death of their father Jacob, the patriarch Joseph's brothers feared that he would seek revenge on them for their earlier treatment of him. But Joseph forgave them, and in one of the clearest explanations of why God permits evil, said to them, "You meant evil against me; but God meant it for good, to bring it about that many people should be kept alive, as they are today" (Gn 50:20).[8] In declaring the feast of Saint Joseph, the Sacred Congregation for Rites made the connection between the two Josephs in this regard:

> As almighty God appointed Joseph, son of the patriarch Jacob, over all the land of Egypt to save grain for the people, so when the fullness of time had come and he was about to send to earth his only-begotten Son, the Savior of the world, he chose another Joseph, of whom the first had been the type, and he made him the lord and chief of his household and possessions, the guardian of his choicest treasures.[9]

The lesson here is one of humility, of sticking close to God in the low moments as well as the high. One of the fourth-century Desert Fathers, Abba John the Dwarf, once asked, "Who sold Joseph?" One of the brothers answered, naturally enough, "It was his brethren." John corrected him: "No, it was his humility which sold him, because he could have said, 'I am their brother' and have objected, but, because he kept silence, he sold himself by his humility. It is also his humility which set him up as chief in Egypt."[10] Joseph could have clung to his status as a son of Jacob, explaining to the traders that he was the brother of the men attempting to sell him (and not a slave captured in combat) and avoided being sold into slavery. But he didn't cling to his lineage, accepting slavery instead, and ended up being raised up as lord over Egypt.

Likewise, Pope Leo XIII pointed out that Saint Joseph, "of royal blood, united by marriage to the greatest and holiest of women, [and] reputed the father of the Son of God," nevertheless "passed his life in labor" and "bore the trials consequent on a fortune so slender."[11] When you consider everything we saw in the previous chapter about his creative courage, remember that he was doing this without money to spare. This is another easy-to-miss point in the Nativity story. The angel greets him in the dream as "Joseph, son of David," in honor of his royal lineage (see Mt 1:20), and Saint Luke likewise stresses that Joseph is of "the house and lineage of David" (Lk 2:4). But this man of Davidic lineage is working as a carpenter, and when he and Mary go up to the Temple for the presentation, they offer "a pair of turtledoves, or two young pigeons" (Lk 2:24), the sacrifice prescribed under the Law for the family that couldn't afford a lamb (Lv 5:7). He and Mary raise Jesus in Nazareth, a town so bad that one of Jesus' disciples would later wonder, "Can anything good come out of Nazareth?" (Jn 1:46). Instead of clinging to his royal lineage, Joseph was content to accept the lot of a laborer and even a refugee in Egypt.

Both Josephs then, point forward to Jesus, who, "though he was in the form of God, did not count equality with God a thing to be grasped, but emptied himself, taking the form of a [slave], being born in the likeness of men" (Phil 2:6–7).[12] Part of the angel's message to Mary was that the coming Messiah would restore the royal fortunes of his family: "The Lord God will give to him the throne of his father Da-

vid, / and he will reign over the house of Jacob for ever" (Lk
1:32–33). But this was to be accomplished through humility,
as Mary recognized in her praise of the God who "has put
down the mighty from their thrones, / and exalted those of
low degree" (Lk 1:52). Because of Christ's humility, God has
"highly exalted him and bestowed on him the name which
is above every name, that at the name of Jesus every knee
should bow, in heaven and on earth and under the earth,
and every tongue confess that Jesus Christ is Lord, to the
glory of God the Father" (Phil 2:9–11). Precisely because he
didn't cling to his divine sonship to avoid suffering, Christ
was able to redeem the world through the Cross and is now
exalted as Lord of heaven and earth.

This is the paradox of Christianity, and it is a paradox
modeled by the two Josephs. In their humility, they were
willing to take the lowest place at the table until God elevat-
ed them, that they might be "honored in the presence of all,"
for "every one who exalts himself will be humbled, and he
who humbles himself will be exalted" (Lk 14:10, 11).

For centuries, Saint Joseph was content to live in humble obscurity in the life of the Church. Perhaps it was important that he remain in the background for so long. Dr.
Mark Miravalle has argued that Marian devotion grew only
slowly in the early Church because "the divine primacy of
Jesus Christ" needed to be established in theology and worship "before any subordinate corresponding devotion to his
Mother could be properly exercised."[13] Likewise, perhaps
Christians could not fully appreciate the role of Joseph as
a husband and father until the theological and spiritual realities of Jesus' virginal conception and divine sonship were
first made clear. But now, in a world in which both the structure of the family and the dignity of workers are threatened,
God seems to be exalting Joseph to a higher place, that we

may learn from him what it is to be a Christian father, disciple, and saint. Pope Benedict XVI has encouraged each of us to look to Joseph, whatever we may be facing: "If discouragement overwhelms you, think of the faith of Joseph; if anxiety has its grip on you, think of the hope of Joseph, that descendant of Abraham who hoped against hope; if exasperation or hatred seizes you, think of the love of Joseph, who was the first man to set eyes on the human face of God in the person of the Infant conceived by the Holy Spirit in the womb of the Virgin Mary."[14]

This is what it means for Christians to "go to Joseph": Whatever the particular circumstances we may be facing, we can find in Saint Joseph both a model and an intercessor. We should both look to him for his example and ask him for his prayers. It therefore seems fitting to conclude with the prayer to Joseph offered by Pope Francis at the close of *Patris Corde*:

> Hail, Guardian of the Redeemer,
> Spouse of the Blessed Virgin Mary.
> To you God entrusted his only Son;
> in you Mary placed her trust;
> with you Christ became man.
>
> Blessed Joseph, to us too,
> show yourself a father
> and guide us in the path of life.
> Obtain for us grace, mercy and courage,
> and defend us from every evil. Amen.[15]

PRAYER

At the end of each of the previous chapters, I shared a pre-written prayer (usually shared with us by a saint) written to Saint Joseph. But at the close of this book, I want to share something slightly different: an invitation to pray to Saint Joseph in your own words. Here's how Saint Josemaría Escrivá puts it:

> In human life, Joseph was Jesus' master in their daily contact, full of refined affection, glad to deny himself to take better care of Jesus. Isn't that reason enough for us to consider this just man, this holy patriarch, in whom the faith of the old covenant bears fruit, as a master of interior life? Interior life is nothing but continual and direct conversation with Christ, so as to become one with him. And Joseph can tell us many things about Jesus. Therefore, never neglect devotion to him — *Ite ad Ioseph*: "Go to Joseph" — as Christian tradition puts it in the words of the Old Testament.
>
> A master of interior life, a worker deeply involved in his job, God's servant in continual contact with Jesus: that is Joseph. *Ite ad Ioseph*. With St. Joseph, the Christian learns what it means to belong to God and fully to assume one's place among men, sanctifying the world. Get to know Joseph and you will find Jesus. Talk to Joseph and you will find Mary, who always sheds peace about her in that attractive workshop in Nazareth.[16]

What made Saint Joseph such an amazing saint? That he was keenly attentive not only to what God was doing externally in the life of Jesus, but to what God was doing *internally*, in those places (like his dreams) which no one else could see. Talk to him about whatever those things, external and internal, are in your own life, and see if you don't end up growing closer to the Virgin Mary and, through her and Joseph, to Jesus Christ himself.

QUESTIONS

1. What is the Holy Spirit revealing by the parallels between the patriarch Joseph in the Old Testament and Saint Joseph in the New Testament?

2. Why has the Church "rediscovered" Saint Joseph after so many centuries of virtually neglecting him?

3. What is one particular way in which I can live more like Joseph today?

4. As I "go to Joseph," what are the particular graces and mercies that I want him to obtain for me through his prayerful intercession?

Notes

THE HIDDEN SAINT

1. Francis L. Filas, *Joseph: The Man Closest to Jesus* (Boston: Daughters of Saint Paul, 1962).

2. John XXIII, Greetings of His Holiness Pope John XXIII to the Members of the Diplomatic Corps after the Midnight Mass (December 25, 1960), accessed February 10, 2021, Vatican.va.

3. John XXIII, *Le Voci*, March 19, 1961. Unofficial English translation available at Oblates of St. Joseph, accessed February 10, 2021, https://osjusa.org/st-joseph/magisterium/le-voci/.

4. Filas, *Joseph*, 528–38.

5. "The Cult of Saint Joseph," in *The Catholic Fortnightly Review*, ed. Arthur Preuss, vol. 14, no. 8 (Techny, IL: Society of the Divine Word, 1907), 397.

6. John Bossy, *Christianity in the West: 1400–1700* (Oxford, UK: Oxford University Press, 1985), 10. See also Ian Boxall, *Matthew through the Centuries* (Hoboken, NJ: Wiley Blackwell, 2019), 47–48,

noting that "the image of Joseph the aged cuckold, rather than Joseph the Just, recurs regularly in the western dramatic tradition," that Joseph was often depicted as an extremely old man, and that his "advanced age is often combined with hints of incompetence."

7. Tom Richardson Pitts, "The Origin and Meaning of Some Saint Joseph Figures in Early Christian Art," Ph.D. dissertation, quoted in Philip W. Jacobs, *Joseph the Carpenter: His Reception in Literature and Art from the Second to the Ninth Century*, History of Biblical Interpretation Series, vol. 5 (Blandford Forum, UK: Deo Publishing, 2016), 15.

8. Mary Clayton, *The Cult of the Virgin Mary in Anglo-Saxon England* (Cambridge, UK: Cambridge University Press, 2002), 145.

9. See Isabel Iribarren, "The Cult of the Marriage of Joseph and Mary: The Shaping of Doctrinal Novelty in Jean Gerson's *Josephina* (1414–17)," in *Individuals and Institutions in Medieval Scholasticism*, ed. Antonia Fitzpatrick and John Sabapathy (London: University of London Press, 2020), 253–68. Despite Iribarren's description of the devotion to Saint Joseph as a "doctrinal novelty," her own scholarship (and Gerson's explicit witness) point to its being a continuation of truths long believed but rarely celebrated.

10. Filas, *Joseph*, 220.

11. Iribarren, "The Cult of the Marriage," 254.

12. John XXIII, *Le Voci*.

13. See Joseph F. Chorpenning, "Saint Joseph in the Spirituality of Teresa of Ávila and of Francis de Sales: Convergences and Divergences," in *The Heirs of Saint Teresa of Ávila*, ed. Christopher C. Wilson (Washington, DC: Washington Province of Discalced Carmelites, 2006), 123–40.

14. Francis, *Patris Corde*, accessed February 8, 2021, Vatican.va.

15. John XXIII, *Le Voci*.

PATRON OF THE UNIVERSAL CHURCH

1. Rick Jones, *Understanding Roman Catholicism* (Ontario, Canada: Chick Publications, 1995), 112.

2. Markus Tilp and Sigrid Thaller, "Covid-19 Has Turned Home Advantage into Home Disadvantage in the German Soccer Bundesliga," *Frontiers in Sports and Active Living* 5 (November 2020), doi: 10.3389/fspor.2020.593499. Their study found that home teams won 54.35 percent of games before filled stadiums, and only 44.10 percent of games before empty stadiums.

3. "From the time of Saint Irenaeus (d. A.D. 200) a necessity for clarifying the biblical case for Christ's human as well as divine nature, notably in combat with gnostic heresies, caused Christian apologists to draw attention to the significant place of Mary in salvation history." David Lyle Jeffrey, "Mary, Mother of Jesus," in *A Dictionary of Biblical Tradition in English Literature* (Grand Rapids, MI: Wm. B. Eedrmans, 1992), 489.

4. For a brief history of the conflict over Nestorianism, see William A. Jurgens, "Nestorius," in *The Faith of the Early Fathers*, vol. 3 (Collegeville, MN: Liturgical Press, 1979), 201ff.

5. The same is true today: The person who claims that Mary *can't* be sinless because "all have sinned" (Rom 3:23) or who says that Mary is inferior to John the Baptist because "among those born of women there has arisen no one greater than John the Baptist" (Mt 11:11) is inadvertently making an equally good argument against Jesus. After all, he, too, was "born of woman" (Gal 4:4). The simplest answer is that both Romans 3:23 and Matthew 11:11 are being taken dramatically out of context, as is clear from their respective contexts. Jesus goes on to say, "He who is least in the kingdom of heaven is greater" than John (see Mt 11:11).

6. Pope John XXIII discusses this history in *Le Voci*.

7. The Sacred Congregation of Rites was the Vatican office responsible for the Liturgy and the predecessor to the modern Congregation for Divine Worship and the Discipline of the Sacraments.

8. Sacred Congregation of Rites, *Quemadmodum Deus*, unofficial English translation, December 8, 1870, available at Oblates of St. Joseph, accessed February 10, 2021, https://osjusa.org

/st-joseph/magisterium/quemadmodum-deus/.

9. Ibid.

10. Francis, *Patris Corde*.

11. Steve Manskar, "The First Disciple: Mary of Nazareth, the Mother of Jesus," *Discipleship Ministries* (blog), December 17, 2017, accessed February 10, 2021, https://www.umcdiscipleship .org/blog/the-first-disciple-mary-of-nazareth-the-mother-of -jesus.

12. Ibid.

13. The Church Fathers "realize that Mary is the type of the Church, not as a mere 'foreshadowing' (as the types of the Old Testament foreshadow the truth of the New Covenant), but as an archetype, that is, as the perfectly, unsurpassably realized 'Idea' of the Church." Hans Urs von Balthasar, "The Marian Mold of the Church," in Joseph Ratzinger and Hans Urs Von Balthasar, *Mary: The Church at the Source* (San Francisco: Ignatius Press, 2005), 141–42.

14. Manskar, "The First Disciple."

15. This is not to deny either the fact that we can also speak of the Church in the sense of the faithful "from Abel" or, on the other hand, that "the wondrous sacrament of the whole Church" emerges as the New Eve "from the side of Christ as he slept the sleep of death upon the cross" (CCC 766). The flock that God had been preparing throughout salvation history is brought to a new visibility in the Incarnation, and it is then molded and shaped into the Church by Christ, before being "made manifest to the world on the day of Pentecost" (CCC 1076). Christ speaks of this gathering of the faithful into the flock of the Church when he says, "I have other sheep, that are not of this fold; I must bring them also, and they will heed my voice. So there shall be one flock, one shepherd" (Jn 10:16).

16. Leo XIII, *Quamquam Pluries*, accessed February 10, 2021, Vatican.va, par. 3.

17. Second Vatican Council, *Lumen Gentium*, accessed February 10, 2021, Vatican.va, par. 11. Pope Benedict XVI has pointed out that

"the Holy Family is the icon of the domestic Church, called to pray together. The family is the domestic Church and must be the first school of prayer." Benedict XVI, General Audience (December 28, 2011), accessed February 10, 2021, Vatican
.va. Pope John Paul II said of the Holy Family, "The Church deeply venerates this Family, and proposes it as the model of all families." John Paul II, *Redemptoris Custos*, accessed February 10, 2021, par. 21.

18. Flavius Josephus, *Antiquities of the Jews*, bk. 17, chap. 6, trans. William Whiston (Bridgeport, CT: M. Sherman, 1828), 28.

19. Francis, *Patris Corde*, no. 5.

20. Leo XIII, *Quamquam Pluries*, August 15, 1889, par. 6. Text of the prayer contained immediately after the text of the encyclical.

21. Pius XI, *Divini Redemptoris*, accessed February 10, 2021, par. 81.

THE MOST CHASTE SPOUSE

1. Larry D. Pickens, "Your View: Christmas Represents God's Life-Giving Light," *Morning Call*, December 25, 2019, accessed February 10, 2021, http://www.mcall.com/opinion/mc-opi-christmas-day -oped-20191225-uc5a5mmvbvfc3lfcn32nbnawoa-story.html.

2. Marge Steinhage Fenelon, *Imitating Mary: Ten Marian Virtues for the Modern Mom* (Notre Dame, IN: Ave Maria Press, 2013), 23.

3. "Full Text: Sister Dede Byrne's Speech at the 2020 Republican National Convention," *Catholic News Agency*, August 26, 2020, accessed February 10, 2021, www.catholicnewsagency.com/news /full-text-sister-dede-byrnes-speech-at-the-2020-republican-national -convention-71435.

4. "There are subtle differences among the terms 'engagement,' 'betrothal,' and 'spousal.' The latter two have more legally binding implications for both of the couple and there is more public ceremony involved in betrothal and spousal. … However, all three could be, and can be, private agreements." George P. Monger, *Marriage Customs of the World: From Henna to Honeymoons* (Santa Barbara, CA: ABC-Clio,

2004), 118. None of these three terms accurately captures the ancient Jewish *kiddushin* or the ancient Greek *ekdosis*.

5. In John 8:41, after Jesus tells the Pharisees that they aren't true sons of Abraham, they respond by suggesting that Jesus is the one "born of fornication." The charge is obviously false, but it shows the level of shame involved.

6. Origen responds to this claim in *Contra Celsum*, I:32, trans. Henry Chadwick (Cambridge, UK: Cambridge University Press, 1952), 31–32. For more on the history and prevalence of this claim, see Ralph Martin Novak Jr., *Christianity and the Roman Empire: Background Texts* (Harrisburg, PA: Trinity Press International, 2001), 79–80.

7. The "bachelor pad" is a relatively recent phenomenon. See James Hay, "Helping Themselves: Men and the Kitchen," in *Cultural Pedagogies and Human Conduct*, ed. Megan Watkins, Greg Noble, and Catherine Driscoll (New York: Routledge, 2015), 97–98. The author argues that "the heyday of the bachelor pad" didn't occur until after *Playboy* began promoting the idea in the late 1950s as a space of male freedom and libertinism.

8. If her father was dead, the man had only three months, rather than a year.

9. The history of the *kiddushin* and *nissuin* are recounted in Anita Diamant, *The New Jewish Wedding: Revised and Updated* (New York: Fireside, 2001), 167. The Greeks (including Greek-speaking Jews in Judea) had a similar two-stage wedding process with the *engýesis* and *ékdosis*. See Uri Yiftach-Firanko, "Judaean Desert Marriage Documents and 'Ekdosis' in the Greek Law of the Roman period," in *Law in the Documents of the Judaean Desert* (Leiden: Brill, 2005), 81. The author says that "*ekdosis* was the only attested Greek act of marriage not only in Egypt, but also in the Greek documents from the Judean desert."

10. Rabbinical texts suggest that this was more common in Judea (where Jesus was born) than it was in Galilee (where he grew up). Michael L. Satlow, *Jewish Marriage in Antiquity* (Princeton, NJ: Princeton

University Press, 2001), 167.

11. *Kiddushin* 2a. This also explains why later questions about whether Joseph and Mary "consummated" their marriage are anachronistic: sex was one way, but not the only way, of creating a true marriage in Jewish culture.

12. The two rabbinical schools at the time, Shammai and Hillel, disagreed about what to make of a couple who slept together *without* intending to marry, and particularly whether it was necessary to give a bill of divorce in such a case. B. *Gittin* 81b. This may help to explain 1 Corinthians 6:16. At the time it was written, a man who slept with an unmarried prostitute was then considered to be married to her!

13. See *Shulchan Aruch Even HaEzer* 26:1.

14. Lynn Cohick, "The Real Problem with Mary's Baby Bump," *Christianity Today*, December 18, 2009, accessed February 10, 2021, https://www.christianitytoday.com/ct/2009/decemberweb-only /real-problem-with-marys-baby-bump.html.

15. This is also why it's confusing and misleading that even many scholars refer to the *kiddushin* as the "betrothal." The couple was legally wed, could have sexual relations resulting in legitimate children, and needed a divorce to separate. In every way except cohabitation, they seem to have been like an ordinary married couple. Referring to them as "engaged" or "betrothed" would be as inaccurate as referring to a couple on their honeymoon as merely "engaged" until they return home.

16. John MacArthur, *The MacArthur New Testament Commentary: Matthew 1–7* (Chicago: Moody Press, 1985), 22.

17. I explain the Emmanuel prophecy, and the way that Mary and Jesus fulfill it, in much greater depth in chapter three of *Who Am I, Lord? Finding Your Identity in Christ* (Huntington, IN: Our Sunday Visitor, 2020).

18. Dan Lioy, *David C. Cook NIV Bible Lesson Commentary* (Colorado Springs, CO: David C. Cook, 2010), 135.

19. Charles R. Swindoll, *Swindoll's Living Insights: Matthew 1–15*

(Carol Stream, IL: Tyndale House, 2020), 30.

20. This twofold meaning exists both in English and in the underlying Latin. See Walter W. Skeat, "Pure," in *An Etymological Dictionary of the English Language*, hereafter *Etymological Dictionary* (Mineola, NY: Dover Publications, 2005), 486. This work gives the definition of *pure* as "unmixed, real, chaste, mere," and traces its etymology from Latin to French to English.

21. The English word holy literally comes from wholly. See Skeat, "Holy," in *Etymological Dictionary*, 275. This is also the sense of the Hebrew.

22. Virginity is also a symbol of an even more important kind of holiness: a soul clinging wholly and completely to Christ. The *Catechism of the Catholic Church* declares: "Mary is a virgin because her virginity is the *sign of her faith* 'unadulterated by any doubt,' and of her undivided gift of herself to God's will. It is her faith that enables her to become the mother of the Savior: 'Mary is more blessed because she embraces faith in Christ than because she conceives the flesh of Christ'" (506).

23. John Paul II, *Redemptoris Custos*, par. 1.

24. Augustine, *Of Holy Virginity*, Nicene and Post-Nicene Fathers, 1st series, vol. 3, *St. Augustine*, ed. Philip Schaff (Peabody, MA: Hendrickson, 2nd edition, 1996), 418.

25. There are typically two objections to this theory. The first is that the evangelists don't mention it. That's true (although Luke 1:34 might imply it), but it's a lot easier to explain why the Evangelists might not mention Mary's earlier vow of virginity than why they wouldn't mention the angel's giving explicit instructions to the couple not to have sexual relations. The second objection is that vows of virginity are a Christian invention. The *Encyclopedia Judaica* claims that "the deliberate renunciation of marriage is all but completely alien to Judaism," and later rabbinical texts argue that "every man is obligated to marry a woman in order to be fruitful, and to multiply," and that the one who does not "is as if he spills blood, and lessens the appear-

ance, and causes the divine presence to depart from Israel." Immanuel
Jakobovits, "Celibacy," in *Encyclopedia Judaica*, Jewish Virtual Library,
accessed February 10, 2021, https://www.jewishvirtuallibrary.org
/celibacy; *Shulchan Aruch Even HaEzer* 1:1.

But it was not always so. The birth of Christ occurred near the
height of the influence of the so-called Essene sect within Judaism. See
John Healy, in *Natural History: A Selection* (London: Penguin Books,
1991), 61n2. He calls the Essenes "a religious sect, or brotherhood,
which flourished in Palestine from the second century BC to the
end of the first century AD." Although small in number (maybe four
thousand adherents at their largest), the Essenes' radical renunciation
of worldly pleasure, and their embrace of celibacy as the highest ideal,
attracted the attention of Jews such as Philo and Josephus and even
Roman historians such as Pliny the Elder. Philo, *Hypothetica* 11.14–17;
Josephus, *Antiquities of the Jews* 18.1.5 and *The Jewish War* 2.8.2–13;
Pliny, *Historia Naturalis* 5.15.73. For a discussion of these and other
sources, see Joseph J. DeVault, "The Concept of Virginity in Judaism,"
Marian Studies, vol. 13, no. 6 (1962): 23–40. And the Dead Sea Scrolls
(likely themselves of Essene origin) include a lengthy "Temple Scroll"
that describes the validity of a girl's "promise of abstinence," made in
her father's hearing, if he remains silent. (The Temple Scroll [11QMiq
58], 53:16–21.) Some of the difference in attitudes can be seen in Jesus'
teaching (see Mt 19:12), as well as the theology of Saint Paul (1 Cor
7:8–9) and the Book of Revelation (14:1–4), suggests that some (but
not all) believers are called to it as the highest spiritual state. Jesus'
disciples don't appear shocked by the teaching. In fact, it was they who
suggested that "it is not expedient to marry," given the severity of the
Christian view of marriage and divorce (Mt 19:8–10). All of this is
to suggest that celibacy had a place in first-century Jewish life that it
didn't in medieval (or modern) Jewish life.

26. Augustine, *Of Holy Virginity*, 418.

27. Ibid.

28. *Protoevangelium* 9:6.

29. Fulton J. Sheen, *The World's First Love* (San Francisco: Ignatius Press, 1996), 92. Sheen's argument matches the most ancient evidence. The nineteenth-century Italian archaeologist Giovanni Battista de Rossi rediscovered the Christian catacombs and reported that in the art in them, "Saint Joseph certainly appears in some sarcophagi; and in the most ancient of them as a young and beardless man, generally clad in a tunic," and that it is only around the fifth century that artists began depicting him as an old man. Giovanni Battista de Rossi, *Roma Sotterranea*, bk. 2, trans. J. Spencer Northcote and W. R. Brownlow (London: Longmans, Green, 1879), 142.

30. Ibid., 93.

31. Jerome, Letter LXXVII to Oceanus, in Nicene and Post-Nicene Fathers, 2nd Series, vol. 6, *Jerome: Letters and Selected Works*, ed. Philip Schaff and Henry Wace (Peabody, MA: Hendrickson, 2nd edition, 1996), 158.

32. "In stressing the primary *end* of marriage — procreation — certain theological treatises have overlooked the primary meaning of marriage, which is love." Dietrich Von Hildebrand, *Marriage: The Mystery of Faithful Love* (Manchester, NH: Sophia Institute Press, 1997), xxvi.

33. Leo XIII, *Arcanum*, accessed February 20, 2021, Vatican .va, par. 7.

34. Jerome, Letter LXXVII to Oceanus, 158.

35. Thomas Aquinas, *Summa Theologiae*, II–II, q.151, a.1, c.

36. Augustine, *On Lying* 40, in *Lying and Truthfulness*, ed. Kevin DeLapp and Jeremy Henkel (Indianapolis: Hackett Publishing, 2016), 32.

37. Francis, *Patris Corde*, par. 7.

38. Ibid.

39. Second Vatican Council, *Gaudium et Spes*, accessed February 10, 2021, Vatican.va, par. 24.

40. John Henry Newman, *Meditations and Devotions of the Late Cardinal Newman* (New York: Longmans, Green, and Co., 1903), p. 269.

41. Leo XIII, *Quamquam Pluries*, par. 4.

JOSEPH THE JUST

1. Saint Thomas Aquinas, *Commentary on Matthew*, 44.

2. Ibid., 44–45.

3. Ibid., 44.

4. Bill Mounce, "What Is a 'Just' Man? (Matt 1:19)," Bill Mounce, May 7, 2017, accessed February 10, 2021, https://www.billmounce .com/monday-with-mounce/what-%E2%80%9Cjust%E2%80%9D -man-matt-1-19.

5. Pope Saint John Paul II quoted the older preparatory prayers for Mass, which celebrate that this messianic desire was fulfilled (and more) for Saint Joseph: "O happy man, Saint Joseph, whose privilege it was not only to see and hear that God whom many a king has longed to see, yet saw not, longed to hear, yet heard not (cf. Mt 13:17); but also to carry him in your arms and kiss him, to clothe him and watch over him!" John Paul II, Homily of John Paul II at the Shrine of Saint Joseph (June 4, 1997), accessed February 10, 2021, Vatican.va, par. 1.

6. Rick Warren, "If God Is for You, Who Can Be against You?," August 15, 2019, accessed February 10, 2021. https://pastorrick.com /if-god-is-for-you-who-can-be-against-you/.

7. The actual number appears to be less than half of the 365 claimed, even counting in alternate ways of expressing the "fear not" message. See Fr. Felix Just, "Have No Fear! Do Not Be Afraid!" Catholic Resources, October 13, 2020, accessed February 10, 2021, https:// catholic-resources.org/Bible/HaveNoFear.htm; David Lang, "A 'Do Not Be Afraid' for Every Day of the Year?," Accordance Bible, June 22, 2012, accessed February 10, 2021, https://www.accordancebible .com/a-do-not-be-afraid-for-every-day-of-the-year/.

8. Rudolf Otto coined the term because the existing words for religious experience had become too watered down. Words such as *sacred*, *holy*, and *awe*, however, point to the reality expressed by the word *numinous*. See John W. Harvey, "The Expression of the Numinous in

English," in Rudolf Otto, *The Idea of the Holy*, trans. John W. Harvey (Oxford: Oxford University Press, 1958), 216–17.

9. C. S. Lewis, *The Problem of Pain* (New York: HarperOne, 1996), 5–6.

10. The hymn has been part of the Byzantine liturgy since 626, but the philologist Leena Mari Peltomaa argues that it likely dates closer to the time of the Council of Ephesus in 431. Leena Mari Peltomaa, *The Image of the Virgin Mary in the Akathistos Hymn* (Leiden: Brill, 2001)

11. Akathist hymn 3:10, in Peltomaa, *The Image of the Virgin Mary*, 5.

12. Akathist hymn 23:6–8, in Peltomaa, *The Image of the Virgin Mary*, 19.

13. Quoted in John Paul II, "Homily of John Paul II at the Shrine of St. Joseph," June 4, 1997.

JOSEPH, THE FATHER OF JESUS?

1. Thomas J. Craughwell, *Patron Saints: Saints for Every Member of Your Family, Every Profession, Every Ailment, Every Emergency, and Even Every Amusement* (Huntington, IN: Our Sunday Visitor, 2011), 22.

2. Greg Tobin, *Holy Holidays!* (New York: Saint Martin's Press, 2011), 44.

3. John Paul II, *Redemptoris Custos*, par. 7.

4. Augustine, Sermon 51.21, in *Sermons, Vol. III (51–94)*, ed. John E. Rotelle, trans. Edmund Hill (Brooklyn, NY: New City Press, 1991), 33.

5. Augustine, Sermon 51.16, in *Sermons*, 33.

6. See Patrick J. Temple, " 'House' or 'Business' in Lk. 2:49?," *Catholic Biblical Quarterly* 1, no. 4 (October 1939): 342–52.

7. Leo XIII, *Quamquam Pluries*, no. 3.

8. Bernard of Clairvaux, Sermon 19.7, in *Commentary on the Song of Songs*, trans. Matthew Henry (Altenmünster, Germany: Jazzy-

bee Verlag, 2016), 94.

9. John Paul II, *Redemptoris Custos*, par. 7.

10. Leo XIII, *Quamquam Pluries*, par. 3.

11. Benedict XVI, General Audience (December 28, 2011).

12. Paul VI, discourse (March 19, 1966), quoted in John Paul II, *Redemptoris Custos*, par. 8.

13. Leo XIII, *Quamquam Pluries*, par. 3.

14. Benedict XVI, address (March 18, 2009), accessed February 10, 2021, Vatican.va.

15. Francis, *Patris Corde*, par. 7.

16. Timothy Dolan, *Priests for the Third Millennium* (Huntington, IN: Our Sunday Visitor, 2000), 185.

17. Thomas Aquinas, *Summa Theologiae*, I, q.13, esp. a.6.

18. Francis, *Patris Corde*, par. 7.

19. Steven Tracy, "Headship with a Heart," *Christianity Today*, February 1, 2003, accessed February 10, 2021, https://www.christianitytoday.com/ct/2003/february/5.50.html.

20. John Paul II, *Redemptoris Custos*, par. 8.

21. Lenore Skenazy and Jonathan Haidt, "The Fragile Generation," *Reason*, December 2017, accessed February 10, 2021, https://reason.com/2017/10/26/the-fragile-generation/.

22. "A father who realizes that he is most a father and educator at the point when he becomes 'useless,' when he sees that his child has become independent and can walk the paths of life unaccompanied. When he becomes like Joseph, who always knew that his child was not his own but had merely been entrusted to his care." Francis, *Patris Corde*, par. 7.

23. Fr. Roger J. Landry, "The Priestly Life and Witness of John XXIII," April 22, 2014, Catholic Preaching, accessed February 10, 2021, http://www.catholicpreaching.com/wp/wp-content/uploads/2014/03/The-Priestly-Life-and-Witness-of-John-XXIII-Copy.pdf.

24. John Henry Newman, *Meditations and Devotions of the Late*

Cardinal Newman, pp. 269–270.

CREATIVE COURAGE AND
THE SILENCE OF GOD

1. Cf. Tyler Huckabee, "So, Were Mary and Joseph Actually Refugees?" *Relevant*, December 15, 2020, accessed February 10, 2021, https://www.relevantmagazine.com/justice/social-justice/so-were-mary-and-joseph-actually-refugees/.

2. Benedict XVI, Angelus (December 26, 2010), accessed February 10, 2021, Vatican.va.

3. Pius XII, *Exsul Familia Nazarethana*, accessed February 10, 2021, https://www.papalencyclicals.net/pius12/p12exsul.htm.

4. Vivian Cabrera, "Wouldn't It Be Nice if an Angel Told Us What to Do in a Dream?" *America*, December 18, 2020.

5. José Antonio Loarte, "Life of Mary (X): Flight into Egypt," *Opus Dei*, March 17, 2014, Opus Dei, accessed February 10, 2021, https://opusdei.org/en-us/article/life-of-mary-x-flight-into-egypt/.

6. "According to an ancient tradition, Saint Joseph did not take the common road through Hebron, nor the one through Eleutheropolis and Gaza, but he selected the least suspected road through Joppe." A. J. Maas, *The Life of Jesus Christ*, 4th ed. (St. Louis: B. Herder, 1904), 37.

7. Francis, *Patris Corde*, par. 5.

8. C. S. Lewis, *A Grief Observed* (New York: HarperOne, 1996), 5–6.

9. See *Summa Theologiae*, II-II, q.47, a.8.

10. Aristotle, *Nicomachean Ethics*, 1109b4–5.

11. Francis, *Patris Corde*, par. 5.

12. Ibid.

13. Sometimes this relationship is described in terms of the sisters Saint Mary and Saint Martha, with Mary as the contemplative and Martha as the active Christian. But this risks separating contemplation and activity too dramatically. The Virgin Mary and Saint Joseph illus-

trate instead that (whatever the particular states to which we've been called) prayer and action must be intertwined.

14. Excerpt from "The Akathist Hymn in Honor of the Righteous Joseph the Betrothed of the Most-Holy Virgin, Mary," accessed via yearofstjoseph.org/devotions/prayers/.

ITE AD IOSEPH

1. Kerri McCaffety, *Saint Joseph Altars* (Gretna, LA: Pelican Publishing, 2003), 19.

2. Francis, *Patris Corde*, par 1.

3. Francis, Angelus (December 29, 2013), accessed February 10, 2021, Vatican.va.

4. "Joseph, when he had heard these things, was not offended, neither did he say, 'The thing is hard to understand: Didst thou not say just now, that He should "save His people"? and now He saves not even Himself: but we must fly, and go far from home, and be a long time away: the facts are contrary to the promise.'" Saint John Chrysostom, Homily VIII on Matthew, Nicene and Post-Nicene Fathers, 1st Series, vol. 10, *St. Chrysostom: Homilies on the Gospel of St. Matthew*, ed. Philip Schaff (Peabody, MA: Hendrickson, 2nd edition, 1996), 50.

5. Ibid., 51.

6. Benedict XVI, homily (May 6, 2006), accessed February 10, 2021, Vatican.va.

7. This points to another parallel between the two Josephs. While the first Joseph was sent to Egypt to ensure that the sons of Israel would have bread in time of famine, the second Joseph was sent to Egypt to ensure that the sons of Israel would later receive "the Bread of Life and the Food of reason that came down from heaven" to heal the famine of "the lack of truth." See Leo I, Sermon 33, Nicene and Post-Nicene Fathers, 2nd Series, vol. 12, *Leo the Great, Gregory the Great*, ed. Philip Schaff and Henry Wace (Peabody, MA: Hendrickson, 2nd edition, 1996), 146.

8. This is a hallmark of the patriarch Joseph's character. Even after

his elevation, he did not seek revenge on his brothers or on Potiphar's wife (whose false accusation against him had resulted in his unjust imprisonment for two years).

9. Sacred Congregation of Rites, *Quemadmodum Deus*.

10. Quoted in *The Sayings of the Desert Fathers*, trans. Benedicta Ward (Kalamazoo, MI: Cistercian Publications, 1975), 89–95.

11. Leo XIII, *Quamquam Pluries*, par. 4.

12. Many of the Church Fathers, including Saint John Damascene and Saint Ephrem the Syrian, rightly saw the patriarch Joseph's descent and rise as a prefigurement of the death and resurrection of Christ as well.

13. Mark Miravalle, *Introduction to Mary: The Heart of Marian Doctrine and Devotion* (Goleta, CA: Queenship Publishing, 2006), 41.

14. Benedict XVI, homily (March 19, 2009), accessed February 10, 2021, Vatican.va.

15. Francis, *Patris Corde*.

16. Josemaría Escrivá, *Christ is Passing By* (New York: Scepter, 2010), eBook edition.

About the Author

Joseph Heschmeyer is an instructor at the Holy Family School of Faith, and the author of *Who Am I, Lord? Finding Your Identity in Christ* (Our Sunday Visitor, 2020) and *Pope Peter: Defending the Church's Most Distinctive Doctrine in a Time of Crisis* (Catholic Answers, 2020). Previously, he was both a litigator in Washington, D.C., and a seminarian for the Archdiocese of Kansas City in Kansas. He lives in the Kansas City area with his wife and two children.

PATRIS
CORDE

WITH A FATHER'S HEART

APOSTOLIC LETTER
On the 150th anniversary of the proclamation
of Saint Joseph as patron of the Universal Church

POPE FRANCIS

PATRIS CORDE
With a Father's Heart

Pope Francis
$4.95 | 978-1-68192-946-0

In this apostolic letter, Pope Francis reflects on Saint Joseph and his multifaceted role as a father. The purpose of this letter, Pope Francis writes, "is to increase our love for this great saint, to encourage us to implore his intercession and to imitate his virtues and his zeal." Saint Joseph is a beloved father; a tender, loving father; an obedient father; an accepting father; a creatively courageous father; a working father; and a father in the shadows. As protector, advocate, and guardian of the Holy Family, Saint Joseph has always been venerated as a father to all Christians.

Available at
OSVCatholicBookstore.com
or wherever books are sold

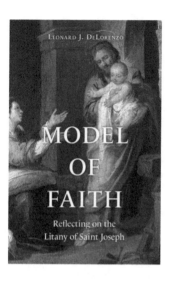

MODEL OF FAITH
Reflecting on the Litany of Saint Joseph

Leonard J. DeLorenzo
$9.95 | 978-1-68192-948-4

Each of the reflections in this devotional focuses on one of the twenty-two names, titles, or honors of Saint Joseph that we encounter in his litany. As we pray to Saint Joseph, offering our petitions to his care, and contemplating his life and his witness, we are drawn into communion with God who yearns to dwell with each of us, and dwelt in this world in the household of Saint Joseph.